LEAVE OUT
THE TRAGIC PARTS

LEAVE OUT THE TRAGIC PARTS

A GRANDFATHER'S SEARCH
FOR A BOY LOST TO ADDICTION

DAVE KINDRED

PUBLICAFFAIRS

New York

PublicAffairs

Hachette Book Group
1290 Avenue of the Americas, New York, NY 10104
www.publicaffairsbooks.com
@Public_Affairs

Printed in the United States of America

First Edition: February 2021

Published by PublicAffairs, an imprint of Perseus Books, LLC, a subsidiary of Hachette Book Group, Inc. The PublicAffairs name and logo is a trademark of the Hachette Book Group.

The Hachette Speakers Bureau provides a wide range of authors for speaking events. To find out more, go to www.hachettespeakersbureau.com or call (866) 376-6591.

The publisher is not responsible for websites (or their content) that are not owned by the publisher.

Print book interior design by Amy Quinn.

Library of Congress Cataloging-in-Publication Data
Names: Kindred, Dave, author.
Title: Leave out the tragic parts: a grandfather's search for a boy lost to addiction / Dave Kindred.
Description: 1st Edition. | New York: PublicAffairs, 2021.
Identifiers: LCCN 2020008031 | ISBN 9781541757066 (hardcover) | ISBN 9781541757080 (ebook)
Subjects: LCSH: Kindred, Jared Glenn, 1988– | Drug addicts—United States—Biography. | Drug addicts—Family relationships—United States.
Classification: LCC HV5805.K56 K56 2021 | DDC 362.29092 [B]—dc23
LC record available at https://lccn.loc.gov/2020008031

ISBNs: 978-1-5417-5706-6 (hardcover), 978-1-5417-5708-0 (e-book)

LSC-C

Printing 1, 2020

There is no grandfather who does not adore his grandson.

—Victor Hugo, *Les Misérables*

If a storyteller thinks enough of storytelling to regard it as a calling, unlike a historian he cannot turn from the sufferings of his characters. A storyteller, unlike a historian, must follow compassion wherever it leads him. He must be able to accompany his characters, even into smoke and fire, and bear witness to what they thought and felt even when they themselves no longer knew. . . . They were young and did not leave much behind them and need someone to remember them.

—Norman MacLean, *Young Men and Fire*

For Cheryl

CONTENTS

AUTHOR'S NOTE

I have never written anything more true than this book. I also have never written anything in which I was less certain of the facts. For reasons made clear in the text, the book's primary on-the-road characters are unreliable narrators. To give their stories clarity and coherence, I have reported names, dates, places, and events as best I could determine them. It was more important to me that the characters told the truth as they knew it. That, I believe, they did.

PREFACE

This is a story about a boy I knew from the week of his birth and a young man I never knew at all. The boy was my grandson, Jared Glenn Kindred, and the young man was Goblin. That was Jared's road name, Goblin. He lived on the street until he learned to hop freight trains and then he lived on the road. He was one of those wanderers whose lives are a mystery and a bafflement, an undoable jigsaw puzzle. To find the light in that darkness, the storyteller goes in search of those who knew Jared who became Goblin. The storyteller who is also the grandfather then writes it truly. He writes it with tears and compassion and laughter. He writes that every time he talked to Jared who became Goblin he ended the conversation saying, "Love you, boy," and every time the grandson said, "Love you too."

Jared was born December 8, 1988, delivered three minutes before his brother, Jacob, fraternal twins, one weighing five pounds, the other five pounds, one ounce. The week before Christmas, I saw the boys in a braided-twig basket, Jared on the left, Jacob on the right. My wife, Cheryl, lifted them out of the basket and placed them in my hands. They stretched from my palms to halfway up my forearms. I wanted to remember how tiny they were. To me, at last, the birth of a child was amazing, a miracle, twice a miracle, Jared and Jacob. To see them was to remember the birth of my son, their father, Jeff. I remembered my wife in labor for hours, begging me to rub her back and, every time I rubbed her back, screaming, "Don't touch me!"

At the birth of our son I was twenty-two and knew nothing. My memory of his birth is a blur of school, job, marriage, the baby's coming, the screaming, and then we went back to work. Cheryl was a day-shift nurse. I was a sportswriter working days, nights, and weekends because, when you're young and hungry and tireless, all you want to do is work and get to where you want to be. Where I wanted to be was not in a labor room with the screaming. I wanted to be out making the future happen. I was a kid myself, and I didn't know the future was happening in that labor room, our son being born.

Then, suddenly, I was forty-seven years old. And our son was a father, and he knew what was happening even if I never knew. Jeff held the twins in his arms and called them "Jake and Jed, my country boys." He looked into the camera, and I'd never seen a prouder dad. Had I ever held our son in my arms and had a picture made? I could search in drawers and boxes and maybe I'd find a picture, but that wouldn't count, because it would mean I didn't remember and the picture must not have meant much to me when it was taken.

I made a fool of myself in love with the grandsons, and I figured I did that because I didn't do it for my son and here was a second chance. Maybe I could show love now and my son would notice and be happy that I'm his dad loving his boys the way I never loved him. Or maybe it would remind him how much he resented the absence of that love. Who knows? We're all guessing. My guess is my son saw in my love of the grandsons a love he never saw for him and somewhere in him there is a mournful bell tolling for the absence of his father's love and that bell never goes quiet.

So I'm the storyteller writing this book about Jared who became Goblin. In every book like this, where the storyteller is lost in the dark and looking for the light, people hearing the story want to know how a father's son and a grandfather's grandson goes to live on the street, where he drinks and finds a way to hop trains across America, where he drinks more. People hearing the story want to know how it happened and why, and the best the storyteller can do is to do what he does, which is find those who knew him, the road dogs who traveled with Goblin, and listen to what they say and how they say it.

Jared's journey put him in a small circle of twenty-first-century hoboes who call themselves "travelin' kids." A buddy of his called their world "an underbelly of America that most people don't even know exists." They get where they're going by any means available. They walk, they hitchhike, they "ride the dog" (a Greyhound bus). Most often, they clamber onto freight trains, which is illegal, dangerous, and, once done, apparently irresistible. In five years, Jared rode trains twenty-five thousand miles.

A line tracing Jared's travels moves through Virginia and the Carolinas into Florida and along the Gulf. It runs to California and back, up to Tennessee, Ohio, and Pennsylvania before turning north to Vermont and south through Massachusetts to New York. He called from Richmond and San Diego, from Boston, Chicago, and Ocala. He loved New Orleans. He paraded in the French Quarter and drank on a Mississippi River wharf by the Café du Monde. There he sang with a crew he named the Scurvy Bastards, raggedy-ass mischief-makers who in another time might have been prankster pirates coming ashore from the Caribbean. He called to say hi or to chatter about his latest adventure. *Naked girls,*

Grandpa, and they're running through the forest, naked. He taught me
how easy it was for a grandpa to wire cash from Western Union. *I
need a Megabus ticket from Albany to the city, $19 is all.* The world
of travelin' kids is at once small and unlimited. There may be only
a couple hundred of them, no one knows, maybe a thousand, no
one cares enough to count them. They live inside no boundaries.
Wherever they are, that's where they want to be.

I'm writing in the service of a storyteller's passion, which is always the same—find a good story and tell it well. I have told a
thousand stories about other people, and those were easy because
everything could be made to make sense. But when it's the storyteller's life and his son's life and his grandson's, it's complicated in
ways unimagined and in ways that no one can know until they are
lost in the dark groping for a way out of the confusion. Still, the
storyteller tries to tell it real and true and the best he can because,
for him if for no one else, there was a need to know what happened
out there. I had to know what happened. I loved the boy Jared who
became the man Goblin who created a life unlike any life most of
us will ever know or want to know, a wanderer's life, not homeless,
for he had homes where he was loved, but a wanderer who slept
on sidewalks and under bridges and along railroad tracks behind
the Jax Brewery in New Orleans. I had to know what happened. I
had loved the child Jared, and when he slept in my bed I told him
sleepy-time stories. I did it because I hoped that someday he would
talk to me about anything and everything in ways my son had never
talked to me, and in ways I had never talked to my father.

Then I lost sight of Jared. Our time together had been counted
in hours; it became minutes. Once upon a time, he would not shut
up; then, silence. Soon enough he became a stranger, still beloved
but a stranger, and then he was gone, and I asked what I might
have done to hold him close and, before him, to hold my son close.

I asked, what if I'd done this, what if I'd said that, a thousand what-ifs, all with unknowable answers. As best I could do it, I had to find out what happened. It's not that I wanted anyone to forgive me. I wanted to forgive myself for not recognizing Jared's pain, not knowing how to help him. Maybe if I could connect the dots and find more dots and connect them all, maybe we would be together again, grandson and grandfather. Could this little book that we've done together, the boy's voice here, his friends telling their Goblin stories, the beautiful ones and the heartbreaking ones, could it bring us together again? I had to know.

There was a time in the sadness that I had dreams, four dreams in a month. In one I am a major league baseball player. I am getting on the team bus for a ride to Yankee Stadium. But I have forgotten my glove. I return to the clubhouse for the glove and reboard the bus. Only now it's a city bus and it's not going to Yankee Stadium. It's wandering through Manhattan, across a river and into Brooklyn, where I get off the bus and stand behind a chain-link fence. I am watching kids hitting dirty baseballs on a muddy vacant lot covered by rocks. They invite me to play. But I don't have a glove. Now I have left it on the bus. "Somebody," I say, "take me to Yankee Stadium," and a tall, skeletal, gray-bearded man wearing catcher's shin guards says, "Get in that taxi." I tell the driver, "I gotta get to Yankee Stadium." The driver is the movie star Meg Ryan. She has a notebook and seems to be a reporter, and I say, "You want a good story? Today's my major league debut and I will not get a single to right field because I am here in Brooklyn." And Meg Ryan says, "Where's your glove?"

In other dreams I lose a golf bag and a laptop, and in one I am lost on the ground floor of a vast, derelict building with slivers of light streaming through the ceiling. It seems to be an abandoned steel foundry. I walk up one of its steel-mesh stairways that casts spiderweb shadows, and I open a giant door and I am blinded by light. I'm now in a church. It's an Anglican church with British people in the pews. They see me and they draw in their breath at the sight of a grimy intruder at their very proper church service. I wonder why I'm there.

I told people about the dreams, and a friend said the dreams were about loss, the loss of things, the losses signifying the loss of Jared. There were more dreams too, and they all had me groping in the darkness, afraid, anxious, unable to do what I needed to do, unable to do what I'd done forever. I came to understand that those dreams were not about loss. They were about the emptiness that follows loss, the paralyzing emptiness of despair.

Someone asked, why tell Jared's story? Why go into the dark, why not grieve and move on? Why write a story that has no answers but only pain and more questions? One answer is, it's a good story. There is that. There is also the friend who said, "You have to tell Jared's story. You have to tell it for him and for yourself. Keep him alive in your heart. Tell his story for his parents, for Jacob, and for all the other kids out there like him. All your love and concern couldn't save Jared, but you might just be able to save some of them traveling the same road. All those kids whose wiring and biochemistry make it impossible to accept the help they need. Tell Jared's story."

I found one of Jared's road dogs, a brute of a girl called Aggro. She talked and I listened to the music in her story, music that Jared would have heard. She said:

Sometimes the best medicine for whatever's bothering us is not a shot or a beer but just taking a ride. Saying, "Fuck it," and jumping on the next thing smoking, no matter which way it's headed. Just sitting back and listening to the wheels clack over the ties, feeling the wind and sunshine on your face, smelling the countryside, rocking with the smooth sway of the train. As the miles roll away, so does all that pain, all that

worry and melancholy, and it's replaced by such peace that the only ex-
planation can be is that it's from God. That's why I ride trains. For
peace of mind that can be found nowhere else. It's like trains take care
of us. They rock us to sleep at night, keep us cool on a hot day, sing to us
when we're feeling down. Some nights you're rolled out in a field and you
hear that train horn in the distance, that lonesome whistle blowing. And
you go, "I hear you, baby. I miss you too."

I found a picture too. It's a picture of Goblin and his road dog
Booze Cop. They are all grime and tattoos, travelin' kids looking
into the camera lens, Booze Cop bare-chested in a ball cap with a
bandanna around his neck, an arm draped over Goblin's shoulders.
I asked Booze Cop about that picture and he said:

We took this picture on Decatur Street in New Orleans. Goblin
musta found that straw hat alongside the road. Not easy to remember
what happens in New Orleans, easy to get drunk in that town. Goblin
looks like a farmer, the bibs, that hat. You're asking what people would
think seeing us? They'd be like, "Get outta here, scum." I look at that pic-
ture and I'm going, "My little brother! Havin' a good time."

I am a grandfather telling a story about his grandson, and I
look at that picture of Goblin and Booze Cop and I think: *Look at*
them. Look past the dirt and the tattoos, and look past the scars of their
lives, those real and those no less real for being unseen. Look again. See
them. Really see them. They are our brothers and sisters, our sons and
daughters, our grandchildren. They are us . . .

I had to know what happened. As a boy, Jared had lived with
us. Goblin, I saw only once and only late in his story. I wanted to
fill the emptiness of loss with a story about the love that comes before loss and lives in me yet.

ONE

I began this story with a name, and not even a name but a nick-name. I heard about a girl who called herself Stray. She had been with Jared on his first train-hopping ride. Doing a reporter's work—rummaging through social media, following threads there, making phone calls—I found her. We talked, texted, and connected on Facebook. To talk with Stray was to know that Jared's story best starts with the adventure, the romance, the light. It starts in front of a drugstore in San Diego, California, in August 2010.

Stray was a wandering waif in patched denims. She needed a drink, so she went to a place where she knew others of her kind would share a half-gallon. She sat in the afternoon sun at that CVS when here came a little guy with a sweetheart's baby face. She noted with respect and admiration that her beautiful hero carried a brown paper bag of the kind you take away from a liquor store. He was in no hurry, shambling up, sure of himself. He wore combat boots with no laces and brown Carhartt bib overalls blackened by railroad grease and made filthy by nights in America's dirt. The

Carhartts hung loose on his frame, no shirt, his shoulders summer-tan. His blond hair went several directions at once. His wide-open eyes were round and blue and alive and kind.

By way of introduction, he said, "I'm Jared Kindred."

"I'm Stray Falldowngoboom," she said.

Jared laughed. "Really?"

"I'm a stray cat. And when I get drunk, I fall down, go *boom*. Call me Stray."

"Cool," he said. "I'm Goblin."

Goblin was twenty-one years old. He had a home, but he had chosen to be homeless, unwashed, unshaven, stinking to high heaven, and broke. He had a red scruff of beard and a crude facial tattoo of dark blue lines that began on his forehead and curled around a cheekbone before ending on the bridge of his nose. He became Goblin the night he sat with a buddy called Booze Cop in a high-dollar mall and panhandled for change. They "flew sign," meaning they held aloft a piece of cardboard with a message. This one, printed with a black Sharpie, read:

ZOMBIES COMING!
NEED CHAINSAW
ANYTHING APPRECIATED

"People look at me like I'm some spooky creature," he said to Booze Cop, and Booze Cop said, "Like a goblin or something."

Stray was tiny, seventeen years old, pale and freckled with blue eyes and rust-red dreads. The day before, she'd gotten sideways with railroad police in Cheyenne Wells, Colorado. They plucked her off a train's coal car, clicked handcuffs on her, and put her on a plane to San Diego. They did that on the notion that the girl's parents, sobbing and grateful, would take the poor child back home and clutch her to their bosoms. The police didn't know that her parents were long divorced and she lived with her mother, who let her quit school in the sixth grade and do whatever made her happy, which in Stray's case meant she was free to wander.

So the mother was fine with her daughter hanging out in San Diego. From there Stray planned to get to Colton, the biggest railroad junction in Southern California, and hop out on the first train she could catch. Waiting at the CVS, Stray told the kid with the brown paper bag, "I've been dealing with weird-ass foster cares in the sticks and cornfields and jail under the sheriff's house in Bumfuck, Colorado."

Jared said, "Need a drink?"

The kid with the homeless, happy, thirsty look said, "Damn right." And she said, "Hellacious tattoo."

"Mom hates it."

"Don't they always?"

He'd flown to San Diego because of the tattoo. On August 3, 2009, his mother, Lynn Ann Sigda Kindred, had called me, the grandfather, sobbing.

She managed to say, "Jared has done the one thing I asked him to never do."

The anguish in Lynn's voice had been frightening. I said, "What happened?" What had he done? Arson, a bank robbery, a car theft, what?

"He has tattooed his face."

Her beautiful child's baby face.

She said, "Hell, I've got tattoos, so I don't mind tattoos."

Crying.

"But his face."

We could laugh about the time Jared went all punk Mohawk, his hair spiked and dyed purple, green, and blue. Teenagers want attention. This was different in degree and kind. The most generous interpretation of a facial tattoo makes it an assertion of individuality and commitment to an artist's aesthetic judgment. Jared's was a fuck-you to the world he would leave and a passport to the world he would enter.

Alcohol was involved when a friend, Craig AntiHero, did the tattoo. Mike Tyson, the former heavyweight boxing champion, may have paid thousands of dollars for a Maori tribal facial tattoo that was a precisely executed work of art. Not Jared. He allowed a buddy off the street to use his face for the first tattoo he had ever done. Craig did what poor folks call "a stick-and-poke." His tools were primitive: a sewing needle dipped in India ink and lashed to a toothbrush, a contraption powered by a small motor removed from a radio-controlled car.

"We had no design in mind," Craig said. "We had a motel room, and I did it there freehand with Jared checking it in a mirror."

The tattoo was fresh in Lynn's mind a year later when Jared told her he planned to go from Virginia to San Diego. A girlfriend had left him, and he was pursuing her.

"Who's driving?" Lynn said.

"Craig."

"*No, no, nooo*," Lynn said. "If you drive across the country with that guy, you'll wind up with tattoos up the yin-yang."

Lynn knew that inside the travelin' kid culture was a clique of tattooed and pierced punk-rockers. The "crusty punks" changed clothes and bathed on an irregular basis, and then only under duress. The final certification of authentic crustiness was a facial tattoo. Jared had gone all in. He was still her child, still Jared under those marks, but her sorrow was in realizing what the ink meant. There was no coming back.

Still, Lynn told me, damned if she would let Jared go three thousand miles in a car with an amateur tattoo artist.

I asked, "What can I do?"

"An airplane ticket?" she said.

And so Jared, having changed from civilian traveling clothes into his travelin' kid's greasy stuff, came to meet Stray Falldown-goboom in front of that CVS. Because he had wandered enough to know what a wandering waif wants, Jared dropped a hand into that brown paper bag and with a flourish brought forth a half-gallon jug of Old Crow.

Stray said, "Exactly what I was trying to get into for the night."

As unlikely as it was that either Jared or Stray had read *On the Road*, they must have felt what Jack Kerouac felt when his man Dean Moriarty slid behind the wheel of their car and gunned the engine: "We all realized," Kerouac wrote, "we were leaving confusion and nonsense behind and performing our one and noble function of the time, *move*." Here Jared had a proposition for Stray.

"I want to get to New Orleans for Halloween," he said. "Want to go?"

Suddenly in from Colorado, Stray had no plans other than the usual wanderer's plan of seeing what might happen next. She said, "I'm ready. Let's hit it."

He said, "How we getting there?"

"Colton yard." Biggest in California, one of the biggest anywhere, the starting point for every train rolling east.

Jared said, "What's Colton?"

She didn't laugh. Anybody who'd ask that question was new to the life. She said, "You've never caught out?"

Silent, Goblin sipped at the bourbon, and Stray knew he'd never hopped on a train. Last thing she needed was a newbie. Newbies do foolish things, and foolish things can get you killed on a freight train. But she liked him. She asked about the necklace he wore. Sharks' teeth, he said, put together by his mother, a good-luck thing. Stray liked it and liked his blue eyes and the bird's-nest mess of dirty-blond hair. He had moxie and independence, or else he'd have never let somebody do a tattoo that he knew his mother would hate. Nor was it a small thing that this sweetheart had walked up on her with a half-gallon of Old Crow.

Now, in San Diego, chasing a girl who had bailed on him, Goblin had found another, this Stray, a train-hopper.

"I'm ready to try," he said.

"New Orleans, Louisiana—NOLA—Halloween, here we come," Stray said. "Cemeteries above the ground, all that scary voodoo shit, and drinking by the Mississippi. Forget the bitch here, you'll find a better one there. We got two months to get there. Listen to me. Riding ain't that hard. Just do what I do. Only rule is, don't do anything stupid. Stupid gets you killed. Fall off, best case is you lose an arm or leg. Worst case, you're hamburger."

Together, Stray and Goblin would move two thousand miles in two months, on railroad tracks zigzagging from Southern California to New Orleans. It's not like a storyteller can vouch for it all in the sense of saying, "Damn right, nothing but the God's honest truth." But the way Stray told it, the journey was good and fun, and if it's true that she painted from a full palette of wanderers' glory, so much the better.

Stray's Story

Jared and I would ride together. It was August, so we had two months to get to New Orleans for Halloween. We'd pass through California, Arizona, New Mexico, Texas, Louisiana—you can't believe the shit we saw and did. First thing was a bus from the CVS to Perris.

In the little California town of Perris, on a dusty street in a Mexican barrio, Goblin and Stray watched fights matching people against dogs tethered to heavy chains. Then a midget and a one-eyed man offered them vodka and a proposition.

"What's he saying?" Goblin asked, meaning the midget.

"He says One-Eye wants to rob that liquor store."

Declining both drink and crime, Goblin and Stray hung around long enough to see the banditos walk into the liquor store, walk back out, and immediately be swarmed by a dozen cops.

By morning, the travelers had panhandled change for bus fare from Perris to Riverside and on to Colton. They took a long, miserable hike in 110-degree heat to the yard, stopping only at a grocery store for wine.

In Colton yard, standing alongside a railroad boxcar for the first time, Goblin leaned back to see the roofline. From a distance, a boxcar might look like part of your electric train set, but up close it's a freakin' building. It can be twelve feet high set on wheels three feet tall standing on rails a half-foot aboveground. It can be sixty feet long and ten feet wide. Sometimes it weighs three hundred thousand pounds, maybe five hundred thousand pounds loaded.

Goblin said, "Holy shit."

Stray said, "Come over here."

She led him to a grain car. A grainer is nearly as tall as a boxcar but less terrifying because it has a flat landing at its ends, "porches," each with enough room for a person, a backpack, and a dog. Above the porch, cut into a wall, is a round hole. A rider can crawl in there and escape some of the wind and weather and relentless thunder of a moving freight train.

On that grainer, Stray and Jared caught a short ride to a gully south of Los Angeles where, under a bridge, they met up with

Booze Cop and one of Stray's ex–road dogs, a heroin-addicted eccentric called Feral.

The four rode to Barstow, sharing two half-gallons of vodka that encouraged them to scratch tattoos into their arms and argue about whose was prettiest. At sunset they crawled through a culvert, keeping in mind that Barstow was a "hot" yard full of "bulls"—the railroad security officers charged with enforcing federal laws against train-hopping. Their presence demanded the travelers be, in Stray's words, "considerably ninja." She explained: "We gotta jump about twenty strings of cars now without being seen by man or animal." Once they had squeezed between cars and pulled themselves over the bulky couplings that connected them, the ninjas settled onto another grainer porch. They waited. Then they heard the hiss of air engaging the train's brakes before the line of cars jerked into motion.

The ninjas slept through San Bernardino and woke up in Vernon.

Goblin didn't know shit about what he was getting into. I told him the facts of life as a train-hopper. The first year it's an Adventure. Strange places and strange people. Like this, here we are in the worst stinking shithole in the country. Vernon, California. It's almost as bad as Gary, Indiana. They've got these meat-rendering plants with animal carcasses lying around rotting and spoiled.

I already see that Goblin is different from most travelin' kids. He sure as hell isn't interested in being Billy Badass and one-upping people. Kid's set in his ways, wanted nothing but a good time. Honestly, I love him. This afternoon he jumped over a railing and beat a dude's ass for calling me a dirty whore for digging through his ashtray. So we're not even really started yet and he's showing me some balls.

Off the grainer at Vernon, we walked to City of Industry, a long walk, one side of LA to the other. Walked through Chinatown and East LA, slept in some park, and woke up to sprinklers soaking us. Goblin screamed like a little girl.

A four-day trek. We spent most days hiding from rain under a trestle by dead tracks, drinking vodka, and waiting to make our move. Feral disappeared a day or two, but he's now back riding with us, Feral being this guy who I count as a maniac spirit talking satanic shit. One night he's shooting up heroin and he's out, like, he's straight-up dead. Goblin and Booze Cop start splashing water on him—and he comes to life. Dy-amn.

We had no business hopping out while it was pouring. Even warm summer rain, when you're sitting on a piece of metal going fifty miles an hour, will chill you to the bone. Waiting around, we made decent money and shaved the sides of our heads in the reflection of a CD, done out of boredom and drunkenness.

Our hop-out spot was just off the main road in a ditch, covered in roaches. (LA is dirtier than all hell.) Goblin played with the roaches like pets. He kicked at the vermin and they'd scatter, and I would scream and run across the street. He got a damn kick out of it. We had a good time ruining each other's good time. What're road dogs for, right?

Finally, we made our move, jumped a southbound on the fly, and again scored another shitty porch ride, and started hauling ass out of LA to Yuma, Arizona, where we slept that night in a parking lot by a liquor store.

We flew sign all the next day for booze and went to the Mexican market downtown and grabbed steaks since Booze Cop's food stamps were on. Grilled by the river and swam all day in the deadly heat. I'm talking 120-something. You jump in the water and walk out and in two minutes you're dry.

We spent the next five nights in Yuma, bouncing back and forth be-
tween new Yuma and old Yuma.

Waiting in Yuma, Stray and her crew settled by the Colorado River and swam to escape the desert's blast-furnace heat. They were stripped down to underwear when two cops showed up.

"We're looking for whoever stole a purse downtown," one said.

"Do we look like we've been downtown?" Stray said.

Once the cops moved on, the crew went downtown. There they found an intersection that they hoped would restore them to the prosperity necessary to buy two half-gallons of bottom-shelf vodka and steaks for the evening's meal along the river. At the intersection, they flew sign to catch the attention of charitable-minded motorists. Stray's best sign:

MOM SAID WAIT HERE
THAT WAS 7 YEARS AGO
SPARE CHANGE?

On the fifth night by the river, a kid named Marcos disappeared. He was a refugee from El Salvador they'd picked up in Los Angeles. On the theory that anyone from El Salvador should be suspected of something, Booze Cop called him "The Terrorist." Someone sent Marcos out for food. He returned with water and tamales. An hour later, during dinner, someone said, "Where's The Terrorist?"

Goblin had seen him walking toward the river. "He was, like, moaning, and saying, 'No más, no más.' What's that mean in Mexican?"

"He's from El Salvador," Booze Cop said.

"Same thing."

"Means 'no more, no more.'"

They never saw The Terrorist again. Maybe he walked into the river until he couldn't walk out. Or maybe his few days on the road cured him of train-hopping and he turned toward a bus station. He left behind, on the riverbank, his worldly goods, a hospital bag containing pants and a pair of shoes—evidence enough, as Stray put it in a eulogy of sorts, that "some people are not cut out for this life."

They moved camp to a ditch under Yuma's historic Ocean-to-Ocean Bridge and waited another day for an eastbound freight. When one rolled up, it was a string of "suicides": cars with no floors, only edges about as wide as a body. Stray said, "We're heading east on the first train we can catch, and this is it, all suicides. Scary as fuck. You ready, my little Goblin buddy?"

"Yep," he said, adding, "maybe," and he reached up to touch his mom's lucky necklace of sharks' teeth.

"Nice to do riskier shit once in a while," Stray said. "Makes you feel like your life is actually worth all this bullshit."

With three weeks to go before Halloween, they left Yuma and blew through Tucson. Goblin was loving it.

Rolling across New Mexico, he danced in a gondola, an open-topped railroad car with low sidewalls. It was a night in summer. He sang Billy Idol's "Dancing with Myself." The train rolled east along the southern edge of New Mexico. It moved through mountains in the moonlight, and in an open railroad car the boy danced, arms and legs flying every which way. Cool, crisp air rushed over the gondola's sidewalls and lifted dust and scraps of rust from the car's floor. The boy danced in the night and sang, "If I had the chance, I'd ask the world to dance." In the moonlit shadows of the mountains, the freight was coming into El Paso, Texas. The city had its lights on. The boy was dancing. How he could dance, no one knew, for as always he had had much too much to drink.

Before dawn, on the hillsides of Juárez, Mexico, the riders saw Border Patrol guards with semiautomatic rifles. Northeast they rolled, past Odessa toward Dallas and Fort Worth, headed for New Orleans because New Orleans is heaven for travelin' kids. It's practically illegal to be sober on the city streets, and diners at fancy restaurants hand out their white-box leftovers. Goblin and Booze Cop had been there many times, but they'd always arrived by car, driving or hitchhiking, bumming their way.

They'd never done it like this, never by train. Goblin had called home and said, "Mom, so cool. We're going, like, fifty or sixty and everything's shaking and I was dancing. All the noise, after a while it sounds like violins." It was steel wheels on steel rails, the cars squeaking, metal-on-metal screeching, screaming, and in the violence the boy heard violins accompanying his dance. The beast of a moving freight train tosses riders against its steel, beating them with thunder and wind, screaming through the night. Then, slowing down, passing industrial plants and electric towers, there's a glimmer of light ahead. Night gives way to color and the train coasts into a yard. Riders grab their backpacks, hop off, and run to avoid the bulls.

They'd done five weeks of desert heat and railroad grime and unforgiving noise and a lake's worth of vodka. They'd seen a dozen cops come down on a midget and a one-eyed guy in a Mexican barrio. They'd seen the maniac demon creature Feral snap back from the dead. They'd seen, or not seen, The Terrorist drown himself in the Colorado River. Though each day's travel carried Goblin east, toward home, he was now as far from home as he had ever been. He had dared to do what he told his father he would do. He would leave and be gone forever. Stray dared him to ride suicides, and by damn he'd already decked a guy who insulted her, he would for sure ride suicides with her.

He told her, "I'm in. I'm going to die before I'm thirty anyway. I might as well have fun doing it."

They came to White Settlement, Texas, a Fort Worth suburb. That day, off the train and panhandling on a city street, Stray and Goblin made a discovery unfamiliar to travelin' kids. A cop can be a human being. They weren't certain of that until, stopped by a patrolman walking his beat, they decided to entertain him with what Stray called "our wet-brained stupidity and strange lifestyle choice." The cop brought out his video camera to capture the travelers "singing GG Allin songs and acting wing-nut for his amusement, hoping it would buy us a get-out-of-jail-free card. Sure enough, he got off on our witty retorts and tone-deafness and gave us a bunch of coupons and a free pass to make whatever money we needed and then please leave the city's streets safe for the civilian population."

Afterward, Stray called an old friend, Dee, an Asian, her first road dog, and now a stripper, and told her, "Four of us just climbed off this steel death-ship machine. We're looking to get housed up for a couple days."

"Honey, you came to the right place," Dee said.

The place had no electricity, no water, no nothing. Goblin, Feral, and Booze Cop brought in six half-gallons of vodka despite Stray's warning that even a little alcohol would make Dee "go batshit crazy." Which it did. For no apparent reason other than the shenanigans seemed inevitable, Dee did a striptease, screamed in Japanese, danced in dizzying circles, and closed the show by throwing acrylic paint all over the walls. That performance set off a funhouse melee with everyone face-slapping paint on everyone else. Soon enough, Goblin and Booze Cop found themselves turned upside down by the naked Dee, whose unseen attributes included a black belt in karate. At night's end, the boys wore paints of many colors.

First thing the next morning, Stray's crew caught out on a freight running north and east and moving them 217 miles to Texarkana. They rode in a "Viking ship," a car with a porch that was big enough for all of them but also presented the terrifying possibility of sliding down the car's side wings onto the track and under steel wheels turning at fifty miles per hour. A sudden storm dumped rain on the riders as they moved fifty-seven miles south, to Jefferson, Texas, where they disembarked by a bridge that crossed a lake and swamps. Soaking wet, tired of the cold, covered in chiggers, isolated by floodwaters, drinking cheap vodka for three days, they slept under that rickety, rusting-steel bridge. Slept? With eighteen-wheelers roaring overhead all night? *Clink clank clunk bang bang, BANG BANG screeeeeech bang BANG.* On the fourth morning, to preserve an ounce of sanity and a gram of dignity, the crew chose to walk through a swamp rather than endure another night of death-metal cacophony. They soon spotted a McDonald's. "Civilization at last," Stray said.

She announced they would next move to Shreveport, fifty-five miles south and east. There they hiked five miles into the city center, slogging through swamplands while the demon creature Feral scared Goblin with every step, telling him the swamp's alligators could crawl up on the shoulder of the road and the bastards ran so fast on those short little legs that they could snatch off a hitchhiker's leg before he saw the thing coming. For all the five miles, Goblin walked in the exact middle of the road. By the time they got into town, Feral needed to feed his addiction and split off from the group to find crack, Stray tagging along. Goblin and Booze Cop left the pair a note, "See ya in NOLA," which was another 327 miles southeast. Jared and Booze Cop moved from Shreveport to Baton Rouge and on to New Orleans, hopping off at the Gentilly yard, six miles north of the Café du Monde, a long, happy walk for the boys who had left Los Angeles two months earlier and come more than two thousand miles. That night Goblin and Booze Cop met up with Stray, Feral, and another dozen travelin' kids on a Mississippi River wharf.

The bonds you make out here are thicker than blood. It's a family. We accept each other for who we are, no matter how weird it gets. Jared and me, we were together under bridges, drinkin' bottles, rollin' down the track, reminiscing life and times, and that's what you get, true family, living life with a person on an everyday basis, not just on occasion. Next time I saw Jared was on the wharf in New Orleans. Two months we'd been on the road. He saw me, gave me that great big gorgeous smile he's got, and he asked, "Got any Old Crow?"

On the wharf, there was bottom-shelf vodka and someone had a guitar, and the motley crew gathered cheek to cheek on the wooden steps in the chill of the night. They were homeless and happy, and Goblin snuggled against an old girlfriend named Lyndzy, a sprite from Asheville, North Carolina. She wore her hair in dreads, and they looked so much alike she might have passed for a sister he didn't have. She had left home and an alcoholic father, looking for anyplace and anyone else. Lyndzy was fourteen when she walked into a liquor store and heard a clerk ask, "Are you looking for your parents, little girl?" She said, "If they cost $12.95 and live on the bottom shelf, yeah, I'm looking for my parents."

Lyndzy first met Goblin in Savannah, Georgia. She thought he was "cool and smart and sweet and goofy." They'd done a lot of hitchhiking together up and down the East Coast and across to New Orleans before losing touch. Now he had chased a different girl to San Diego and circled back to NOLA just as Lyndzy had rolled into town. As always, she drifted to the wharf for good times with old friends. There she saw Jared and shouted, "Goblin!" They embraced and she stood back to say, "Fuck me! Goblin, that tat! I love it! Maggie, come here, you gotta see this."

Maggie was Lyndzy's road dog. Over Lyndzy's shoulder, Goblin saw her and didn't move his eyes off her. She was small and pretty with faint tattoo lines on her cheekbones. She carried a mandolin. The instrument was an iridescent green that sparkled in the night's flickering light. Not often on the road do you see a pretty girl with a mandolin. Jared would remember her if he saw her again.

"I'm Goblin," he said to Maggie.

"Yeah, I heard Lyndzy," Maggie said.

Whoever had the guitar played a chord, and Maggie lifted her green mandolin into place, and Jared and Stray and all the travelin' kids sang the song they lived by, no hip-hop for them, but a rousing rendition of the hoboes' national anthem:

In the Big Rock Candy Mountains
You never change your socks
And the little streams of alcohol
Come trickling down the rocks
The brakemen have to tip their hats
And the railway bulls are blind
There's a lake of stew
And of whiskey too
You can paddle all around it
In a big canoe
In the Big Rock Candy Mountains

TWO

Jared's story begins more truly not inside the thunder of a freight train in the southwestern night but on a soft, silent summer evening when Lynn Ann Sigda came to my desk, upstairs at our house in Georgia, where the windows were open and a breeze moved across the room carrying the sweet smell of magnolia trees.

I was writing. I was always writing. By Lynn's account, she had been standing by my desk for some time, waiting, before she dared speak.

At last she said, "Can I interrupt?"

"Oh, I'm sorry," I said. "What's up?"

"Is it okay with you," she said, "if Jeff and I get married?"

The next words spoken were ones I had never imagined saying. "Sure," I said, "and I hope you have twins tomorrow, a boy and a girl."

Me, a grandfather? Really? I wanted it that much? Me? Grandfathers are old, decrepit men. They're not young, strong guys like me. They get called Gramps. I never knew my grandfathers.

Dad's dad died young, long before my birth. Mom's father had been kicked to the curb, and I saw him only on the street outside Grandma Lena's tavern when he sneaked me a dime for ice cream. Being a father was hard enough. A grandfather? Someday maybe, when I was really old and had time to kill between whittlings. Yet here was a girl who'd come to Georgia to ask us—Cheryl and me—if she might marry our son. And before I understood what was happening, I was imagining the fun of what could come next.

Jeff and Lynn were married in April 1986. I remember the day in the way that workaholic sportswriters remember important life events. It was the Sunday of the Masters golf tournament. I had covered every Masters for twenty years. That day, however, as the father of the groom, I knew nothing of the Masters until I turned on the television at eight o'clock and heard, "Jack Nicklaus today shot a sixty-five to . . ." Which caused me to say, "Oh, shit." Nicklaus had created Masters history by winning, at age forty-six, one more major championship.

I have recovered from that collision of life events—mostly because I liked Lynn. She had been one of those Kewpie doll gymnasts bouncing around in imitation of Olga Korbut, the Russians' 1972 Olympic darling. To say Lynn loved some derring-do is to underestimate her sense of adventure. At twenty-five, she rode motorcycles, tended bar, answered to "Hey, Tiger," and had spent a month in jail for selling weed to an undercover cop. "Damn narc entrapped me," she said. "He begged me for weeks until I found a source."

There was also the day she swam into a river to save some cats. Her fellow workers at a seafood restaurant along the Occoquan River in suburban Washington, DC, saw a man stop his car on the Route 123 bridge and drop a cardboard box over the railing. They saw it splash down and then saw cats flailing in the water.

They did what anyone would do if they knew Tiger. They started shouting, "Hey, Tiger, Tiger! Do something!" They knew she was the resident cat lady, with six of her own at home. They also knew she would do something.

In the water about halfway to the cats, Tiger realized she was well dressed for serving customers but not for swimming. "My jeans were getting heavy," she said. The cats—a mother and three kittens—had caught onto a concrete pillar in midstream. She handed two to a man in a boat, then began swimming back to shore with the other two. Worn out, she thought to ask for help. Not that she often asked God for anything. She believed in God, she just didn't make a big deal out of it. But there comes a time when God comes to mind, and this was such a time for Tiger, who remembered saying, out loud, "God, please don't let me drown. I haven't had any babies yet."

Lynn later told me the cat-rescue story as preamble to the day's news: "Remember what you said when I asked if I could marry Jeff? It's happening. A boy and a girl."

A second sonogram corrected the record. It would be two boys. We drove to Virginia the week after their birth. Jared and Jacob were wrapped in blue swaddling blankets and turned face-to-face in their basket, their hands touching. Jared's hands, tiny as they were, suggested my father's thick carpenter hands. Cheryl placed Jared and Jacob on my arms, and I took them into my heart forever.

The next day a friend called.

"Gramps," he said, "it's nine o'clock. Shouldn't you be having your milk and cookies and be headed for bed?"

"Tom," I said, "it's amazing."

For the first time, I understood what a miracle life is. Yes, I was a father and I'd held my son that way. Hadn't I? Surely I had held my son in my arms just as I held my son's sons. But I had no memory of such a moment. I was twenty-two years old then, a kid myself. Me, a father? That wasn't on my list of ambitions, and yet there it was. But now? A grandfather? A miracle, twice over—those babies were proof certain of life's wonders. I looked down on them, tiny and perfect, one on each arm, and I prayed they would find joy forever and ever, amen.

A grandfather? Me? Hooray. Beyond putting me in the presence of miracles, the babies gave me a second chance of sorts at fatherhood. I was a newspaper reporter and columnist, home only when I couldn't find a story, always writing or thinking about writing, absent in every room even when present. Maybe I could get life right as a grandfather. I indulged myself in imaginings of life with the grandsons. I would see Jared and Jacob fall and rise. They would kick ground balls and drive in winning runs. They would read Shakespeare, rock with Springsteen, and chase pretty girls until the right one caught them. To cradle my son's sons on my arms was to imagine a world without end, for the twins would be eighteen when I was sixty-five and they would be sixty-five with grandchildren of their own when I was gone. Of course, because writers write, those imaginings were put to work in my column. For Christmas Day, seventeen days after their birth, I wrote that Jared and Jacob "had made it healthy through the first daring steps of a long journey that will be full of hope and peril, sadness and joy."

I began a campaign to bring Jeff, Lynn, Jared, and Jacob to Newnan, Georgia, a lovely little town just south of Atlanta. The stars were aligned. Across the street from us, a house was for sale. The Ford dealership in town needed a mechanic, Jeff's dream job. On Virginia's gray, chilly, rainy days, I called my son and daughter-in-law to report that it was bright and warm on our pool deck. Later they would say they moved south because, as first-time parents, and with twins besides, they thought they might need help. It's just as likely they moved so Gramps would shut up about it.

We had moved to Newnan four years earlier. I had been the *Washington Post*'s sports columnist in the Hollywood years when the newspaper was so famous that Robert Redford and Dustin Hoffman made a movie about its Watergate reporting, *All the President's Men*. Some of the *Post*'s glow rubbed off on me in a way that caused the *Atlanta Journal-Constitution* to offer me a job. One of my *Post* bosses thought to end such conversation by invoking prestige. "There's psychic income here," he said. "You move with the heavy hitters."

When the Atlanta managing editor, Ed Sears, came to DC, we met at a hotel so fancy it had a woman in diaphanous white finery, apparently an angel, plucking at a harp in a high alcove in its luncheon room.

I asked Sears, "Did you hire the harpist?"

"Wish I'd thought of it," he said.

The day I decided to leave the *Post*, that psychic-income-preaching boss came to my office door.

"Bad for you," he said, "and bad for the paper."

"Just something I felt I had to do."

"Yeah, like the Baptist preacher following the call of God to more money," he said, as if the poor, pitiable *Post* were some going-broke rag. Maybe a decade earlier, I had asked Red Smith, my hero and the best sports columnist ever, why he had never written a memoir. "I'm saving it in case I get fired," he said. I expected a laugh. There was none, and I decided that if Red Smith worried about the future, I ought to worry too.

So we traded the nation's capital for the county seat of Coweta County. Cheryl was happy to get out of Washington. "Everybody thinks they're so damned important," she said. Newnan had its share of self-important people. But when the mayor's name is Gandy and he drives around town in a Cadillac with a deer-hunter's stand attached to the grill, it's the kind of important that can be tolerated. The mayor also had a possum etched into a tooth, an etching he requested in a moment of envy after a fishing friend showed off a molar with a trout.

You couldn't go farther south than Newnan and get any more southern. In the DC suburbs, Cheryl and I had never met a neighbor. In our first week in Newnan, a young woman from across the street studied a picture of Abraham Lincoln on our living room wall. "It's okay, I guess," she told Cheryl. "Y'all *are* Yankees."

That summer I watched a Ku Klux Klan rally on the courthouse square and asked an old black man about the chrome-handled revolver shining at his belt. "Had 'er a long time," he said, and I counted that as his opinion of the Klan. I never met Scout's sainted Atticus Finch in Newnan, but I did imagine her Boo Radley in every shadowed corner. I quickly learned that the Civil War—known in Newnan as "the War of Northern Aggression"—was a fresh wound. A store clerk once turned down my $50 bill. "We don't take that here," she said even as she took the bill bearing the likeness of Ulysses S. Grant. Our neighbors included a corporate lawyer, a portrait artist, a professional photographer, two airline pilots, the mayor of Newnan, and Miss Lillian, a skeletal old bat in a ratty house dress who thought to spy on the invading Yankees from behind a stop sign at the corner of College and Wesley Streets.

We lived three blocks from the town square. Our house was a Victorian with a wraparound porch that could have accommodated a Confederate encampment. Rising above the roofline, a spire topped a turret room. The house was too ostentatious by half and too expensive even before considering the money-pit problems that come with a structure a century old. We hadn't been looking for a castle. But now that it had found us, we moved in.

Cheryl and I were forty-two years old. We felt like we were starting over.

We met in high school. She had moved from the next town over and immediately became the prettiest girl in Atlanta High School. She was also a member of the National Honor Society. I say I "met" her because surely we met in a school that had only twenty-eight students in its senior class. I just don't remember meeting her. I mean, what would I have said to a smart, pretty girl? I knew batting averages, not girls. I would never have said a word if my sister, Sandra, hadn't insisted I ask Cheryl for a date. I guess I did, and it likely involved a 19-cent ticket to the Palace Theater followed by a milkshake at Louie Deuterman's restaurant next door. I have no memory of a date, though I do remember a moment. The other night, a lifetime later, the moon reminded me of that moment. I had gone out for a walk. It was a warm night in August. The moon, a half-moon, sat high behind thin clouds. On that kind of night, in 1958, I first asked Cheryl if I could kiss her.

The next spring, a matchmaking English teacher, Clarice Swinford, cast Cheryl and me as the romantic leads in our senior class play, *It's a Great Life*. Cheryl was a debutante, I was a doctor. In the last scene, we kissed. (Extracurricular rehearsals became mandatory.) A great life: Cheryl became my wife, the mother of our son, a renovator of historic houses, and the charge nurse in a locked men's ward at a private psychiatric hospital. (Think *One Flew over the Cuckoo's Nest*.) A great life: We walked up the steps of the Lincoln Memorial, and we had dinner in the Eiffel Tower. We drank tea in London, wine in San Francisco, and beer in Munich. We slept in Zürich, Madrid, Rome, and Stockholm. We saw the ovens at Dachau and Michelangelo's *Pietà* in Rome. We lived in

Illinois, Kentucky, Virginia, Maryland, and Georgia, each of our homes made distinctive by Cheryl's work, taste, and eclectic style that she called "Early Barn." All of it was done with common sense, uncommon decency, and an inexhaustible tolerance of my failings.

One more thing about that extracurricular rehearsing.

There was a night in the front seat of my '53 Chevy. As I often did, I talked about my heroics as a high school basketball player, for I was a point guard before the term was invented. Our Atlanta Redwings were undefeated en route to twenty-nine victories.

At last Cheryl had heard enough. "I play basketball too," she said.

"Oh, really?"

"For our church team."

I made my first mistake. "Were you a good player?"

"I scored all our points the other night."

For my second mistake, I asked how many points.

"Fourteen."

My third mistake came in asking a future sportswriter's natural question. How many points did the other team score?

"Seventy-two," she said.

I laughed out loud, which was my fourth mistake, and it was a very bad mistake. It was such a bad mistake that it was my last mistake of the night because the atmosphere in the car turned chilly and by her actions Cheryl notified me that it was time for me to take her home, like right now, please.

Three years later, in the greatest comeback of my career, we got married.

Workaholic, did I say? Always writing? For $5 at an auction, my mother had bought a portable Royal typewriter for my fifteenth birthday. I sat with the magical machine at our kitchen table, waiting, and waiting more, waiting to make my first typed words memorable. Finally, hunting and pecking, I spelled out the name of my baseball hero, the great St. Louis Cardinals hitter, S-t-a-n-l-e-y F-r-a-n-k M-u-s-i-a-l.

The writing became a blessing and a curse. A newspaper promotion ad showed me in a tuxedo with a foot on a suitcase. The ad asked, "Who Writes His Way Around the World?" I was out there so often, gone from my wife, my son, and my home, that I mailed back postcards signed "The Phantom."

From the 1960s to the mid-'90s, flush with monopolistic profits, newspapers spent money on the editorial product. A sports columnist was always on the road for the next big event: Super Bowls, college football bowl games, World Series, heavyweight championship fights (I did ten of Muhammad Ali's), Final Fours, Olympics (summer and winter), Wimbledon, the four major golf tournaments, America's Cups, the Goodwill Games in Moscow (3:00 a.m. changing of the guard at the Kremlin), NASCAR, Indianapolis 500, the Triple Crown horse races (Secretariat at Belmont, beauty in flight). I did all those along with the everyday columns on local teams and subjects. Not to mention nine books.

On our fiftieth wedding anniversary, someone asked how Cheryl and I had made marriage work.

She laughed. "I think it's because he was home only ten of those years."

Our Newnan home soon became Jared's and Jacob's, filled with their toddler energy and chatter. On arrival in Georgia, they were a year old. Soon they moved from walking to running, from babbling to talking, from infancy to childhood. They crawled under our kitchen chopping block and rode tricycles along College Street. We walked with them to the candy store on the court square, where Jacob said, "Peppermint patties, please." At the fire station two blocks away, Jared explored every corner every day, always remembering when he left to say, "Bye-bye, fireman . . . bye-bye, fire truck . . . bye-bye, fire boots."

Jacob liked to "cook." He'd sit on the kitchen floor and extract a dozen pots and pans from the cabinets. Then he'd make "pancakes" by dropping ice cubes onto a skillet and sliding the skillet into an "oven" that to lesser chefs appeared to be the open space between the four legs of the chopping block. There is a photograph of the boys in diapers, standing in front of our Wurlitzer 800 jukebox. Jacob is inspecting the bubble tubes. Jared is spread-eagled on the floor to peer under the machine; we entitled that picture "Elvis, are you in there?" Jacob once sat on my lap through fifteen songs. "He didn't want to quit," I wrote in a journal of that year. "And every time I relaxed my hands on his sides, he reached for them and put them back. He liked the solid feel, the safety. He loved to be lifted high every time Little Richard sang, 'Tutti-frutti' and howled 'Wowwww!'"

Both boys loved to sit with Cheryl as she read to them. When she finished a story, Jared would say, "Read again." He had heard the Peter Pan story so many times that he recognized the plot. When "Maw-Maw" asked him, "Now what happens?" he'd tell her and say, "Read, Maw-Maw."

We finally had a chance to be a real family. Early in our marriage, with both of us working, we'd missed parts of our son's childhood that we could never recover. Now we hoped to make up some for our absences.

On December 7, 1991, the day before the twins' third birthday, we dressed them for a formal photograph taken by our friend and neighbor Bob Shapiro. Bob's camera loved the boys. They were impossibly adorable, both smiling, both with their blond hair in mullets, both in white-on-white tuxedoes, white shoes, purple cummerbunds, and purple bow ties, each more dashing and with greater swagger than the other. Jared, so cool. Hands in his pockets. Weight on his right foot, his left side loose. The beginnings of a smile. Moves his head forward, eyes inviting you in.

In one run of Shapiro's film, the boys share a stool. In another, Jacob sits at his brother's feet. In a third, Jared whispers into his brother's ear. For two hours, the boys struck whatever poses the photographer asked. They shimmered under the studio's soft white lights. In white shoes against a white floor, they seemed to float above the surface, lifted by happiness. However they changed, for however long they both would live, Jared and Jacob were golden boys in those shutter-click moments.

With Jeff and Lynn our neighbors, sharing the boys with us, those Newnan years were the happiest of our lives.

THREE

Two months after that photo shoot, Jeff asked us over for dinner. If we had dinner, I have no memory of it. Some memories break your heart into so many pieces that those pieces float in the bloodstream to your brain and force everything else out. All I remember of that night is recorded in a sentence scratched into my journal: "Jeff said, 'The real reason we asked you over tonight is to tell you we're moving back to Virginia.'"

To be fair about it—and I have no more desire to be fair about it now than I did then—but to be fair about it, my son's announcement should have been no surprise. Jeff had complained about his job, and Lynn so often found our lovely little town beneath her level of big-city sophistication that she enlisted a neighbor for girls-night-out trips to Atlanta, the center of the southern universe. She once said, "Newnan doesn't even have a bowling alley."

Cheryl and I had considered Newnan our last stop in life. Now our son and his wife wanted to ditch it in favor of a return to suburban northern Virginia. At once furious and brokenhearted, I could not say what I thought, which was, *Fine. Go back to Virginia and don't let the state line hit you in the ass. Go. Send us a postcard for Christmas. Go. Go bowling twice a night. Go. Just leave Jared and Jacob here.*

Losing the boys was the dagger in our hearts. My favorite picture was not the Shapiro portrait. It's one Cheryl made with a Kodak disposable camera. Jared, Jacob, and I are at the breakfast table. I'm reading a newspaper. The boys are in blue pajamas. Jared sits on my lap, Jacob sits on the table. I wanted nothing more than to spend the rest of my life reading the newspaper with them. That night, after a dinner I didn't eat, I was maybe five beers deep into pouting before falling asleep. Cheryl cried all night.

On a morning two weeks later, as Jeff and Lynn dealt with movers, Jared came to me and said, "Upstairs." I thought he was confused—did he want to go back to bed? Cheryl whispered, "M&Ms." I had a gumball machine in my office filled with the candy. So we took him upstairs, with Jacob hurrying to catch up. But instead of M&Ms, the boys wanted to sit on my lap at my desk, as they'd done so many times. "Paw-Paw, turn on 'puter," Jared said, and we typed together one last time.

By then Lynn had come upstairs. "C'mon, boys," she said. "We're going to Virginia."

Jared turned to Cheryl. "You come with me?"

Cheryl said, "I can't, honey. I'm going to miss you boys."

Jared might have seen a tear. He asked his grandmother, "Are you going to cwy?"

She said yes, and Jared said, "I cwy too."

I can see the boys still, in our driveway, sitting in their van, ready to leave Newnan. Lynn hugged me and said, "I love you, Paw-Paw." That infuriated me. She was so oblivious to my pain that she could go for affection by using the boys' nickname for me. I pulled away and went into the house, where Jeff was waiting.

He said, "I'm just so sorry, Dad." Crying, he hugged Cheryl and me. "I'm sorrier than you know. One of the crazy things was Lynn got upset over the garage." We had built a garage for his mechanic's tools and equipment. "She was afraid that you, me, and the boys would do things together and leave her out." What the fuck? Jealous of a garage? Jeff said, "We'll get back to Virginia, and I'm going to make it better—or it's going to get worse." I didn't know then what that meant, and I didn't care. I knew only that it couldn't get much worse for us.

In the van, Jared was strapped into his car seat. He stared out a window, forlorn. Jacob was alongside him. As Jeff backed the van down the driveway, Lynn waved from the passenger-side window. She was all smiles.

ooooo

Five years later.

It got worse. Jeff and Lynn went through a nasty divorce. The only consolation for Cheryl and me was that Lynn conceded custody of the boys to Jeff. At the time, I wondered how a mother could give up her only children. And I wondered about what damage, if any, it would do to them. Jeff soon remarried and started a second family with his wife, Lisa, who gave birth to a son, Kaleb, and a daughter, Josie.

And what did Cheryl and I do? We bought a farm in Locust Grove, Virginia, fifty miles south of Jeff's home. Then we built him a house on our land. Again, we had persuaded our son and his family to live next door. Yes, we had replicated the Newnan conditions that had led to sadness. But I was brilliant in creating rationalizations for doing what pleased me. I thought we represented an island of stability in their shipwrecked lives. That, and we simply loved being around Jared and Jacob.

Jared often stayed overnight with us. I talked him to sleep with stories about boys who grew up to be heroes. My nightly cast of a sportswriter's characters included Pee Wee Reese, Muhammad Ali, and Pelé. Jared practiced his knuckle-down shooting after hearing that Pee Wee had been a marbles champion before becoming the Dodgers' shortstop. I told him I once climbed into bed and interviewed Ali under the sheets to get away from a crowd in his hotel room. "Muhammad took my notebook," I said, "and wrote down the names of people in his entourage and how much he paid them a week." Jared, learning to play soccer, liked the story about the poor boy who kicked a ball made of rags. "Tell me Pelé," he said, and we went in our imagination first to Brazil and finally to the Meadowlands stadium, where I heard the greatest soccer player ever, in the last game of his career, shout to the 75,646 spectators, "Repeat after me: Love . . . Love . . . Love."

There was a night in Virginia when Jared sat on my lap and said, "Grandpa, you ever seen that commercial? Y'know, the hair-grow one?"

Grandpa arched an eyebrow. "No, why?"

Jared rubbed his hand across my head in a place once covered by hair.

He said, "Ohhhh, gee, I dunno."

The imp was seven years old.

ooooo

Jared was eleven in the summer of 2000. I was in Montana on a Missouri River canoe trip with my sister, Sandra. Off the river, I called Jeff late one night, just to check in.

He said Jared and Jacob had been fighting and it was awful, what the brothers did to each other on an everyday basis.

"We can't take any more of this," Jeff said. "They won't quit."

"Jeff, do you know the golfer Curtis Strange?" I asked. Strange had won the US Open golf championship twice. He fit into this conversation because he was an identical twin. "Curtis told me that his biggest fight with his brother, Allan, was at the dinner table, and it wound up with food splattered against the ceiling. Jeff, they were sixteen years old. The boys are eleven. They'll figure it out. Give them time."

"No, damn it," Jeff said. "They're just out of control, and they're scaring Lisa too, with what they're doing."

"Like how?"

Jeff said, "Jacob the other day hung Jared by his ankles over the loft railing. Jared wasn't scared. He thinks it's fun, like a kid would. But it could be bad, and Lisa's worried."

Then Jeff cut to the chase. "We're splitting them up. It's Jared who's scaring Lisa the most. He's going to go live with Lynn."

I didn't believe it was happening again. Eight years before, our son had blindsided us with an announcement that he would leave Georgia and take his family to Virginia. Now this? This was crazy. This time, rather than burning in furious silence as I had so long ago, I said, "Jeff, you can't be serious."

The idea was beyond understanding. Following their divorce, Jeff and Lynn had been at war. And now he was sending a boy he said he loved to live with a woman he said he hated? I said, "You can't do that, Jeff. Come on, you can't split 'em up. You can't split up brothers, let alone twins."

"That's what we gotta do," Jeff said.

"Jeff . . ."

He cut me off with a guttural shout. *"I'm the parent here!"*

What son speaks to his father that way? Mom and Dad had survived a depression and a world war and knew the rest of life was the time to smile. They made my childhood warm, comfortable, and safe. About five o'clock, I'd stand at a kitchen window waiting to see Dad's truck coming home from work. We'd sit together to watch television—baseball, boxing, wrestling, *Gunsmoke*. But we didn't talk much. He was Dad! If he spoke, I said maybe a word in reply. Shouting at him was unthinkable. Where had I failed that my son could attack me—those words were an attack—with such vehemence?

I slammed down the phone. For years after that moment, Jeff and I never had a meaningful conversation about the boys. The silence was a mistake then, and a mistake later. During the years when Jared had disappeared into the dangers of the road, a father and grandfather might have teamed up to help him; instead, we shared nothing.

As frustrating and maddening as all that was for a grandfather, it had to be confusing for Jared, eleven years old and ordered to live away from his father and brother. It was one of several unsettling circumstances in his preadolescent years. Following his parents' divorce, Jared lived with one parent or the other but never with both. He was moved from our property in rural Virginia to Lynn's high-rise apartment in suburban Washington. Then, when Jared was seventeen, Lynn left for South Carolina. Jared wanted to stay at his familiar high school rather than become a stranger in South Carolina. Reluctantly, he returned to Jeff's place in Locust Grove and there finished his senior year in school.

Jacob remembered the uncertainty of living with his mother in three different apartments and with his father in two cities. "As soon as Jared and I made friends somewhere," he said, "we moved again."

During those years, the boys began drinking.

"We went to Key West for an uncle's funeral," Jacob said. "Jared and I drank a pitcher of beer by ourselves." They were thirteen years old. "And we drank all through junior high. One night, I remember, we were drunk as shit on beer, but as soon as we walked in the house we snapped right to sober for the five minutes until we got out of sight. Ninth, tenth grade, we did a handle of Captain Morgan." A "handle" is what drinkers call the jug handle on a half-gallon of the captain's rum.

Cheryl and I knew nothing of that, nor did we have any reason to suspect the boys were drinking until one day Jared said, "Grandma, I'm an alcoholic." Cheryl was startled and told me what Jared had said. We let it pass, though, because what could a fifteen-year-old know about being an alcoholic? Maybe a beer now and then, what teenager hasn't done that? But an alcoholic? No way.

We were happy to see Jared on the weekends when he came from the city to the Virginia countryside and his father's house, next door to ours. Jeff had become a Civil War reenactor, one of thousands of men who re-create the war's lives and times. Jared loved the costumes. From time to time, he went to war with his dad, first as a drummer boy and later as a cook.

One of Jared's favorite reenactments involved trains. It took place in Gordonsville, Virginia. During the war, a house there had been converted to a hospital. Jeff and Jared slept in the yard of that house, along railroad tracks that once brought soldiers to the hospital. Jeff said he never got any sleep by those tracks, but somehow Jared slept well.

At best, the boys' senior year was the usual test of teenagers pushing against a father's boundaries. At worst, it was a year of unrest that put them in a home where they felt unwelcome. Jacob's memory of that time was harsh. "Dad said we couldn't live with him after graduation, after we turned eighteen," he said. "He told me to get my shit out of the house, and if I didn't, I'd be picking it up out of the front yard. He said, 'Go join the Marines.'"

○○○○○

After graduation from high school, Jacob came to live with Cheryl and me. Jared was gone. Not to the Marines. Just gone. Somewhere. We knew only that he slept wherever he could find a friend's couch. Then one day he came to our house with the sides of his head shaved, leaving only that punk Mohawk spiked and tinted in purples, greens, and blues. We were clueless. The Jared we had known was shy, quiet, ordinary. Where did this unusual, flamboyant, extraordinary Jared come from?

Maybe the girls knew. We met a Thai American named Nam. We met a soft-spoken beauty, Shannon. A grateful Destiny Lynn King remembered Jared: "I was a freshman at Orange High School when Jared came out there his senior year. I didn't know anybody, and people frightened me. One day, on the bus, I was listening to some music and I had on a jacket that had JESUS FREAK on the back. Somebody tapped me on the shoulder and said, 'What the fuck is a Jesus freak doing listening to Nirvana?' It was Jared. After that, he always protected me on the bus and at school."

Laura Sullivan noticed him. "My friend Ally and I were window-shopping in the Fairfax mall and we saw this kid with that hair and a studded leather jacket and we were, like, *a fellow punk!!* Which was rare in the area. So we started talking to him. We knew the music he liked, bands like Leftöver Crack, Choking Victim, Kevorkian's Angels."

Of the many songs on our Wurlitzer jukebox, none was by Kevorkian's Angels. Where *did* that Jared come from? He had been sent away from our place in the Virginia woods at age eleven. The next six years we saw him only as the occasional weekend or holiday visitor. We seldom saw him during his last year in school, though he lived two hundred yards from us. His life had been turned upside down. On weekends and holidays, he went back to DC to be with his friends. Not only did I not know the punk-rock Jared—I no longer even knew my grandson Jared.

ooooo

Jared slept where he was welcome. With no home of his own, told by his father that he should go join the Marines, he spent one summer in a tent raised by a friend, Chris Allen, who was called Dear God. The tent had room for twelve people under a roof so high everyone could walk around. There was a dinner table inside and a grill outside. The camp sat deep in a ravine alongside I-95 at Fredericksburg, Virginia.

Dear God, Jared, and their cohort lived in the woods, never knowing what came next. Usually the day began with Jared saying, "Dear God, let's go on an adventure." One morning they needed money, so they went to a bank. Instead of driving, because they had no car, they walked. And when they came to the bank's drive-through lane, they became the Dear Godmobile.

"My ex-girlfriend, Tamara, walked where the driver's seat would have been and pretended to be steering," Dear God said. "I rode shotgun and made car noises—*v-room, vvv-RRR-OOOOM*—and Jared was right behind me, in the 'back seat,' lolled over like he had passed out."

The pantomime so amused the drive-through teller that she passed money to the driver, after which the Dear Godmobile walked to the nearest liquor store.

That summer set the course of Jared's life. He met a man who had fallen off a cliff.

Somehow the fall had not killed Michael Stephen. He was blackout drunk when he stumbled through the dark of a forest and fell thirty feet into a rocky gulch. He was twenty-nine years old. He played guitar, wrote songs, and developed conspiracy theories. A child of a broken family, living on the street, he used alcohol and other drugs to self-medicate his pains, physical and psychic. Bruised and broken by the fall into the ravine, Stephen spent weeks encased in splints that immobilized his right leg and left arm.

He slept in an abandoned building in Fairfax, Virginia. There was a concrete post out front, the size of a child's gravestone, with "VDH" etched into it: Virginia Department of Health. The building was a relic of the 1950s, two stories of institutional brick with windows and doors covered by plywood. The building had no electricity and no water, but it did have one virtue valued by squatters: its usable doors could be locked from inside, keeping out all predators, be they thieves or police officers.

For Jared, who had attended schools there, Fairfax was familiar turf. The year in rural Locust Grove was an interruption in the city life to which he had become accustomed. He came to the VDH building with a mutual friend to visit the busted-up guy who was brilliant and bizarre. There he found a place that felt like home, a ghostly hull of a building, and he found a guy, broken by life, who needed help.

Michael's Story

I was drinking myself to death. All alone in that abandoned building. If Jared hadn't stayed, I well may have killed myself or died.

He took care of me. I was in a wheelchair first, then I used a cane. He would help me with everything. It was just me and him for the better part of three months. I don't remember ever feeling quite as safe and content as when it was just the two of us. Just the two of us in the cold, late winter.

My parents split up when I was ten. That's when I started travel-ing. First it was back and forth between Mom and Dad and grandpar-ents. Around nineteen, I started traveling the US. Backpacking. Mostly by Greyhound. Colorado, Washington State, New York, Boston. I hung out with hippies. The "crusty punks" were always trying to start fights. Always smelled really bad. I just got on with hippies better. They had the good pot and the psychedelic mushrooms.

I hardly ever drank. Because when I did, it was a fucking catastro-phe. One day I was blackout drunk at the skate park in Santa Barbara. Apparently, I thought I was Tony Hawk and I grabbed some kid's skate-board and dropped in on a half-pipe. Board came right out from under me and I fell fifteen feet, landing with all my weight on my right side. Broken ribs, painkillers by the mouthful for months, addicted, rehab. Then a girlfriend drops me, steals my savings, five grand that we had marked to buy a conversion van, and she runs off with a guy from her work. I started drinking again.

Kept feeling sorry for myself until I fell off that cliff. Fucking A! Somehow I hadn't broken anything, but my whole body was bruised. My bones were bruised. I was so mad at myself at this point. How stupid can one guy be?

Enter Jared. Just out of high school. I was a grown man, he was barely past adolescence.

I was so angry at the way my shit life was going that I would tell stories of my travels and paint this totally romantic picture of how won-derful the life was. I glorified it all. I glorified my "urban survival skills." I glorified homeless travel, glorified saying, "Fuck it," glorified partying your life away.

He knew nothing about living on the street. He didn't even know he needed water, let alone how to get it. I taught him to stay hydrated. Find a bottle, keep it filled up. If you're hungry, go to grocery stores, they throw away bread every night.

He took it all in, and there was no way he could know how fucked up I was. He was still relatively innocent and naive. I was a prophet of "Fuck It All," and the poor kid became an eager disciple.

He saved my life. And I fed the kid my crazy bullshit. Some friend, eh?

ooooo

Through Jared's time with Stephen on the streets of suburban DC and later on the roads of America, one person kept track of him. His mother.

We had hoped for a daughter after Jeff, and that daughter turned out to be Lynn. As much as it hurt that she and Jeff moved away from Newnan—and as much as divorce added to the pain—I never doubted the one thing that mattered most to Cheryl and me. Lynn loved those boys. After the divorce, she earned our respect by allowing us to love Jared and Jacob the way we had the week they were born. She did that by insisting we share their lives.

In time, I accepted that small-town life in a deep southern state had been a culture shock for Lynn, made more difficult by a failing marriage. I finally understood her good reasons for first giving up custody of Jared and Jacob. Unable to get meaningful work, she enrolled in college and graduated with a degree in accounting. She believed that Jeff's home, with help from Cheryl and me, was the better place for the boys. The decision to leave Newnan had become ancient history best put aside, especially in the boys' tumultuous teenage years. We all celebrated together—Jeff, Lynn, Cheryl, me—on the boys' sixteenth birthday and their high school graduations.

That shared interest soon ended—on Jeff's part. Lynn always knew where Jared was; she demanded that he keep a cell phone with him. In good times, she wanted to hear the happy chirp in his voice. In bad times, she wanted to know how to help. In the really good times and the really bad times, Lynn called me.

Jeff, however, had chosen to be left out of the loop. "The whole time Jared was on the road," Lynn said, "I only called Jeff once to give him any news about our child."

"Why only once?"

"He was so mean to me that I quit calling."

In the cold war of his divorce from Lynn, Jeff cut himself off from any knowledge of Jared's life. I could not do that. I made peace with Lynn. Maybe we were no longer father-in-law and daughter-in-law, but we were in this together. As unlikely as it had once seemed, we became friends, partners, and allies, brought together in common cause for the boy we loved.

FOUR

The trek from San Diego had delivered Jared, Stray, and Booze Cop to the haunted and haunting city of New Orleans. That Halloween of 2010, a band named Widespread Panic played at the "N'Awlins" lakefront. The "Thrilla Guerillas," a flash mob of fifty-seven dancers, slathered on their zombie makeup to do Michael Jackson's "Thriller." Bacchanalia for everyone, orgies of liquid and flesh. Ghosts, ghouls, and goblins—goblins!—paraded down Decatur Street and Bourbon Street, a blasphemous world's holy boulevards. Vampires worked the night, and Jared danced on the roof of the Jax Brewery building, the mighty river a leap away, shimmering in a quarter-moon's light. From atop the Jax building, he saw the lights of Jackson Square and the three spires of St. Louis Cathedral. Best of all, for the moment and for a long time to come, the long journey from San Diego had put Jared in the presence of Christine Maynard.

A freelance writer with a place above a daiquiri shop on Decatur Street, Maynard was the fifty-three-year-old mother of three sons, divorced more than once, a character out of Tennessee Williams, a complicated, suffering, all-enveloping woman given to romance, pathos, tragedy, and tender mercies. In a time of Jared's distress, she would take him in from the street, befriend, nurture, and care for him. This Halloween week, she did him the favor of introducing him to a man whose road name defined him. Puzzles.

Puzzles sometimes worked as an extra in movies made in New Orleans. He was thirty-something, charismatic and troubled, lean and good-looking with ringlets of dark hair. He had HOBO tattooed on the knuckles of one hand, AROUND THE WORLD on the back of the other, and on his ring finger the outlines of a boxcar. For a piece she wrote, Maynard had elicited from Puzzles "lurid details of the pain, suffering, and neglect that he endured growing up. He'd been on the road since fourteen, riding the rails."

With Puzzles, Jared hung out on a wooden wharf at the Mississippi's edge. There was talk of Jean Lafitte and his pirates having walked on that wood. Scurvy bastards they were, someone said. And Jared decided that everyone on the wharf that night, from then on, should be called a Scurvy Bastard.

The first time I talked to Puzzles about Jared, he said, "Goblin had the perfect name."

"'Goblin' was perfect?"

"Kindred," he said. "We were kindred spirits, free spirits. That kid was my brother."

Two weeks after that Halloween, Jared and Puzzles felt the wanderers' need to be in motion. From the Gentilly yard, they hopped out with a girl named Alex Tallent. They were headed west, to San Diego, of all places. On a ride more harrowing than the Stray expedition, the fledgling Scurvy Bastard crew got as far as an Arizona highway.

Alex's Story

Why Goblin wanted to go back where he'd just come from, I don't know. Why didn't matter to me, it was something to do and get out of NOLA for a while.

It was a crazy trip, even before Tucson. Everything that could go right did, and everything that could go wrong did—like with Goblin and Puzzles hopping off in Houston. Goblin was pissed off at my dog, a Jack Russell, Beau, who was acting the fool. Also, we were out of smokes and booze. So Goblin says, "Hey, Puzzles, why not hop off here, fly sign, and make some money?"

We got off way too early, and a bull kicked us out of the yard. It's eighty-something degrees and sticky, and we're carrying our stuff, and we had to walk five freaking miles through Houston's Fifth Ward.

Not everything's clear to me yet, but Puzzles got stung by a wasp, and he had a cut on his leg, and maybe he got beat up. Somehow he wound up in a hospital, and we lost him for the trip.

We got hung up for a week in Houston and met a guy we know, Brock.

○○○○○

On the road, you often are off the road. You can wander into places you shouldn't wander into, and the Fifth Ward in Houston is one of those places. For decades, it was a territory controlled by gangs and drug dealers. The Fifth Ward became the venue for so many murders and the depository for so many corpses that it earned the nickname "the Bloody Nickel."

As Alex and Jared walked from the yard through the Fifth Ward, stray dogs came running at them, snarling, ravenous. The dogs were bad enough. Worse were the small children offering to sell them crack cocaine.

Houston to Tucson took three days. In the middle, in San Antonio, we hopped out, with me and Brock on one porch and Goblin on another porch with a girl we picked up there, a stupid stupid bitch named Jules, who did nothing but chase Goblin's dick.

She had a dog who had parvo, and the only food she had was marshmallow fluff. Marshmallow fluff. Then she ran us out of water because she threw it on her parvo puppy's puke.

And then, all of a sudden, Goblin is gone. The train's breaking up, and we've lost Goblin and the bitch. We hop off and a brakeman says, "What the fuck are you doing out here? It's freezing." Now it's forty-five degrees and windy. So we're asking where the other half of the train is, where our friends are. He says, "Dude, this thing is rolling out in five minutes."

Goblin knows how to get around, so we see him now running after our car, and he's trying to catch out on the fly and he couldn't get on, so we waved him goodbye and knew we'd meet up with him—when, wow, the train stops and he and Jules climb up on a piggyback. Crazy thing about all that is, the brakeman stopped the train for us. He actually drove his truck up to the front of the train and stopped it. Just a nice guy. It happens.

We're out of San Antonio now and past Del Rio near the Arizona–New Mexico border and we get sided out twice—in the desert—with no water, because the bitch threw it all on her dog puke. First time, we're there two hours, four hours, who the shit knows how long? We're dehydrated and we see prickly pears. Goblin says, "Let's get 'em, they got liquid in 'em."

I don't know if you know prickly pears, but they're cactus, and they have these prickly stickers that look like steel needles, and you gotta really be hungry or thirsty to take a bite out of that shit—or at the point of delirium, which we were, so we go pick as many of 'em as we can carry and we devour the damned things.

Second time we're sided out is beside this crappy Latino house, and we see a Mexican lady in her backyard, and we tried to bum a smoke off of her in our broken Spanish. Fumar, por favor? She came back with a giant trucker mug of coffee, a loaf of bread, and a bag of fruit. She was literally the godsend of the whole trip.

And then we get to the Tucson yard, and the bitch Jules is standing up on the grate, exposed to the whole yard, stuffing her pack while we're waiting for the train to slow down. Lo and behold, we see the bull truck driving one train over from us. He's scoping us out because he's seen her, and how couldn't he, it's two frickin' o'clock in the afternoon, broad daylight.

Meanwhile, we're looking for the hole in the fence where we can get out of the yard. Now it's a race to get off the train, find the hole, and get off the property before the bull gets around that other train and gets to us. So we hop off on the fly with our dogs, which can be all kinds of trouble, but we make it okay, and we slide under the fence.

Now there's this highway. We run across one side and there's a median barrier that we'll have to jump over or crawl over, something. We look over it, nothing's coming.

ooooo

On the road, there's always something coming.

So Goblin, Brock, and me crawl up and over the barrier and start running again, running across the highway—when, out of nowhere, going seventy in a fifty-five, there's a car. Smash!

Its mirror clips me on the shoulder and elbow, spins me around. I see Brock flying twenty feet in the air. The car's windshield is gone, he must've bounced off it and destroyed it. His leg is bent, bones sticking out. He's screaming, "Fuck fuck fuck."

I see Goblin writhing on the highway. He'd been hit hard too. His leg is all twisted. The car hit him sideways somehow. Maybe he saw it at the last minute and turned. It hit his backpack first. If not for his backpack, I think he'd have been killed.

ooooo

The hospital report was terrifying. It listed six major fractures up and down Jared's body and cited an "obvious right lower extremity deformity," which meant his leg was snapped below the knee and bent at a grotesque angle. Inside, he had to be a bloody mess: his liver was sliced apart, his bladder ripped open. Somehow, despite being flipped into the air and crashing down on a concrete highway, he had avoided a head injury. Other than that, there was only one exception to the relentless pain he would endure. He made that clear five days later when asked if there was any place that he didn't hurt. He said, "My hair."

The report:

UNIVERSITY MEDICAL CENTER, TUCSON, AZ
Patient: Kindred, Jared
DOB: 12/08/1988
Date of Encounter: 11/20/2010
Age: 21
WT: 66 kgs
HT: 67 inches

This [is] a male pedestrian who was struck by an automobile at 65 mph. He complains of right-sided abdominal and chest pain, which he describes as a constant, sharp pain that is severe and worse with movement. He also complains of right lower extremity pain. EMS notes that the patient has an obvious right lower extremity deformity. He was splinted in the field. The patient is unable to recall the event. EMS notes that he had loss of consciousness on scene.

Patient has a right tibia/fib fracture, right knee effusion, right superior and inferior rami fracture, right clavicle fracture, right pelvic ring fracture, right iliac crest fracture, grade 2/3 liver laceration, intra and extraperitoneal bladder rupture, and multiple abrasions.

Patient gave us telephone number for his mother, Lynn . . .

ooooo

Using Jared's cell phone, a doctor called Lynn and handed the phone to Jared.

"Mom, I got hit by a car," he said.

She asked to speak to the doctor.

"How is he?"

The doctor recounted the injuries.

"Is my child going to live?"

The doctor said yes, and they'd do the surgeries tomorrow.

"I'll be there," Lynn said.

FIVE

On arrival at the Tucson hospital, Lynn asked a nurse, "Where is he?"

In recovery. Surgery went well.

"Where is the recovery room?"

You can't go in there yet.

"Yes, I can."

No, ma'am, he's not out of the anesthesia yet.

"I'm going in there. Now."

Ma'am, we'll have to call security if you do that.

"You damn well better call security, then, because I'm going in there to be with my child."

When a mother who calls herself Tiger flies three-quarters of the way across America and demands to see her injured child, a nurse's appropriate response is to point toward the recovery room and get the hell out of the way. Which explains how, on the day of surgery, Lynn put herself in the recovery room at Jared's bedside and ran a hand over his hair. He had not yet opened his eyes when he said, "I smell you, Mommy."

Not Mom, not Ma. Mommy.

"I'm right here, buddy," she said.

Jared said, "Pinchy-face, Mommy."

He wanted her to do the "pinchy-face" thing she had last done with him as a baby.

Lynn had seen him only once in two years. He came to Myrtle Beach in the summer of 2009, and she saw the facial tattoo for the first time. She didn't like it. She wanted him to erase it, make it go away. Even as he said he would try to remove it, she knew better. He liked the way it looked. After a week, Lynn said, "Y'know, after a while, you don't even notice it. You just see Jared."

Below the tattoo, Mommy pinched her child's cheek lightly.

I had lost track of Jared. I knew he had lived on the street and on the road for most of the three years since his high school graduation. That was not a life anyone could sustain, most likely a life built around alcohol and other drugs. But in a grandfather's denial of what was before his eyes, I preferred to cast Jared's wanderings as a young man's adventure. I had read Twain on Huck Finn "lighting out for the territory ahead." Like Huck, Jared had had enough of where he was and he wanted to be somewhere else.

Lynn called from Tucson. She was not crying. She had seen Jared's mangled body. A tattoo no longer mattered.

Surgeons did two days of work.

Their summary:

UNIVERSITY MEDICAL CENTER, TUCSON, AZ

PROCEDURES/OPERATIONS PERFORMED

11/21—Exploratory laparotomy; repair of rupture.

11/22—Open reduction and internal fixation, right medial clavicle fracture with suture; intramedullary nail fixation, right tibial fracture; open reduction and internal fixation, right pelvic crescent fracture.

He was alive, maybe only because his backpack had come between him and a car. But as broken as he was—he would be in a wheelchair and on crutches through the winter—doctors assured Lynn he would recover. They had put together the pieces of broken bones and sewn together the torn tissue. Time would do the rest, and Lynn was fine with all that.

It was the other thing that worried her more. On her third day in the hospital room, Jared asked, "Why are there two television sets up there?"

Lynn looked at the room's single TV, mounted on a wall, and said, "What?"

"Two TVs, which one am I supposed to watch?" Jared said. "And now there's two of you."

Lynn looked to a nurse.

The nurse said, "He's DT'ing."

Lynn didn't understand.

"Detoxing."

Lynn said nothing.

"Withdrawal," the nurse said. "From alcohol."

The DTs, delirium tremens. In the alcoholic's world, they're also known as "the shaking horrors." They happen when a person addicted to alcohol is deprived of alcohol. For all of Lynn's experience—as a bartender, as a drinker herself—she had never been in the presence of anyone suffering DTs. And this wasn't just anyone. This was the Jared who called her Mommy. At her son's bedside, she had walked into the darkness of his life. What she saw, though she did not yet know it, was addiction. Her baby was an alcoholic.

At 7:52 a.m. on November 27, the Tucson hospital discharged Jared. His "Patient Discharge Instruction & Plan" paperwork came with these sentences:

> Contact PCP [primary care physician] and/or 911 if chest pain or shortness of breath recurs. If any change in symptoms, call your doctor or come to the ER. May use Tylenol as needed. Seek medical attention if symptoms worsen. Take medications as prescribed.

Against all common sense, five days after multiple surgeries across the length of Jared's body, the hospital sent him home. The harsh interpretation of the dismissal is that the hospital needed his bed for someone with a good insurance plan. In that case, the discharge instructions could be read in the world-weary voice of a hospital administrator saying, "We're done with you, kid. Go home, even if you're in pain from top to bottom and can barely sit in a wheelchair. Go home, good luck, and remember, if you really hurt, come to our ER, it's only a transcontinental plane ride away."

"He shouldn't have been on any plane," Lynn said. "They loaded him up with pain meds, morphine mainly." She told the discharging doctor, "If anything happens to my child on this flight, I will kill you."

Security at the Tucson airport searched him. "Every movement hurt," Lynn said. "He kept saying, 'Don't touch me, don't touch me.'" Airline personnel in Atlanta raced his wheelchair through the airport to catch a flight being held. The plane's cabin full of passengers was quiet when he entered—until his wheelchair dropped from the jetway into the plane. The abrupt jostling caused Jared to shout, "Mother-*fucker!*" The waiting passengers applauded his arrival—well and bravely done, albeit profanely.

Though it's never a good thing to be struck by a car going sixty-five miles per hour, Jared's experience could have been an exception. It might take two or three months to recover from his injuries, but in that time he could get sober. He was twenty-one years old. An accident that could have left him dead might have given him a future.

Lynn called me that winter. "A lawyer in Arizona is telling me Jared could have a lawsuit that might be worth $600,000."

The lawyer had proposed a suit against the hospital. He needed Jared to stay in Myrtle Beach for a year, to be available for examinations and depositions. The proposal went nowhere because Jared made it clear he would not, could not, sit still.

"From the start all he talked about was getting well so he could go back to New Orleans," Lynn said. "When we talked about the lawsuit, he said no, he wouldn't do it, the accident was his own fault, not the kid driving way over the speed limit. I explained that it would be against the hospital for kicking him out so quick. They threw him out, and he wasn't ready to go anywhere. The airline wasn't even going to let him on the plane, he looked so bad. But he was so damn stubborn. He kept saying, 'Nope, it was my own fault. And the hospital took care of me.'"

Jared not only argued against a lawsuit, he continued to use alcohol. His only concession was to say he'd stay off vodka and drink beer. Lynn said, "I told him, 'Honey, your little body doesn't know the difference between vodka and beer. It's all alcohol.' But he was convinced that drinking beer was a hundred times better for him than drinking vodka. You couldn't talk to his stubborn ass about that."

When Jared had seen two television sets and two images of his mother in the Arizona hospital, he had revealed undeniable signs of addiction to alcohol. But Lynn had not understood that at the time, nor did I. And now she had missed a second, stronger sign. Jared's "stubborn ass" had nothing to do with his refusal to pursue a lawsuit; the refusal was another symptom of the way alcohol had rewired his brain.

On New Year's Eve 2010, two months after Jared had seen doubles of a TV set during DTs, the addiction made itself evident to Lynn in a prosaic way. Jared had not had a drink since the accident. Lynn agreed to bring him beer. She brought him a six-pack and heard him shout, "That's *not* enough." Six beers would not be enough?

A year off the road would have allowed Jared a full recovery from his injuries. He could have joined Jacob at a community college. He could have built a life alongside his brother and a crew of boyhood friends whose loyalty was fully measured during his recuperation in Myrtle Beach: they drove down from Virginia to celebrate his survival and took him, in his wheelchair, to a strip club.

Jacob tells the story: "Jared was more upset with having to stay in one place than he was with his injuries. He wasn't about staying in one place very long. That's why I and Corey Bean and Levi went down there to see him. At the strip club, he ran out of dollar bills. So Levi gave him a stack of ten bills. Wasn't ten minutes later, Jared said, 'Levi, I need more money.' Levi says, 'What happened to the money I gave you?' Jared says, 'I done gave it to the ladies.' Levi says, 'You gave away $100 already?' He'd given Jared ten $10 bills, not ten ones. Of course, Jared was getting all kinds of free lap dances, being cute and being in the wheelchair. The girls were all going, 'Oh, honey, what's wrong with you?'"

With Jacob and the Virginians at his side, away from freight trains and $12 half-gallons of bottom-shelf vodka, Jared might have recognized the great good fortune of being broken into pieces by that speeding car in Arizona.

But the addiction was more powerful than any possible alternative. Even while in a wheelchair for nearly two months—even after hearing news of eight kids killed in a warehouse fire in New Orleans on December 28, 2010, even when he recognized the firetrap building and some of the dead, even though he knew his own squat, the Pink House, was a disaster waiting to happen—as soon as he could walk, Jared told his mother, he would return to New Orleans.

The addiction demanded to be fed. It wanted to go to New Orleans. It would take Jared along.

Lynn knew little about his life on the road. But she knew she didn't like New Orleans and New York City. "They petrified me," she said. She connected those cities with drug use, particularly heroin. "Jared told me he used heroin but only once because he didn't like it. He said, 'Mom, I drink. I've done coke, yeah, if somebody has it. But no heroin.'"

How ignorant we all were. Lynn's phone calls kept me up to date on Jared's progress after the Arizona surgeries. For a month, then two months and three, he stayed with his mother in Myrtle Beach. It was their longest time together in four years. I thought about his broken body, but not once during that recovery period did I think of addiction. How naive I was, a big-time newspaper columnist, a man of the world (hanging with sportswriters who sometimes couldn't find their way home from the bar), and not once did I think of the real reason Jared wanted out of Myrtle Beach. Not once did I think of flying there to have a conversation about his sickness.

Instead, I liked Lynn's story about a dinner with Jared in late February at Harold's on the Ocean, a beachfront restaurant. "I told him he wasn't going anywhere until he could walk a mile on the beach. I said, 'If you can walk from here to the pier, you're ready to go.'"

Damned if he didn't do it.

Out of the wheelchair in Myrtle Beach, Jared used crutches for two weeks.

Off the crutches, he used a cane.

With the cane, he did the mile.

Took an hour, but he did it.

Lynn was an amateur photographer with an idea for a book. She asked people to write a word on the beach at the Atlantic's edge. She asked for a word representing the one thing they would change about their lives. She took photographs as the tide moved over the words and erased them.

That day on the beach, after he had walked the mile, Lynn asked, "Jared, what would you wash away?"

He used the cane to scratch five letters in the sand.

B O O Z E

What he had never said, what he had refused to say, he had written in the sand.

His mother said, "Really?"

"Yeah," he said.

What Lynn had first seen in the Arizona hospital room without knowing what she had seen, she now saw on the beach and recognized fully. She saw the frightening power of addiction, for even as Jared wanted booze gone, he could not resist it. On February 17, 2011, Lynn did a post to Facebook friends:

Went back to doc last week and he's good to go. Took him a few days to stop using the crutches but he's doing great now. Now he's planning his big escape! Guess being stuck in bed at Mom's for 3 months is all he can take. . . . Wish he would stay but at 22 years old I can't make him do anything. All I can do is be there for him whenever he needs me. Thanks to everyone for your support, kindness and prayers. Neither Jared nor I would have made it through without each and every one of you.

The day he declared himself ready to get out of Myrtle Beach and back to New Orleans, Lynn called me.

"There's nothing I can do to change his stubborn-ass mind," she said.

"Pray," I said.

On March 4, Jared left for New Orleans. He had been in Myrtle Beach 103 days.

SIX

The choice, Myrtle Beach or New Orleans, was no choice. The 103 days at his mother's home had helped Jared heal. They also told him how much he missed New Orleans. Of course he wanted to be there. He was a star in the town's travelin' kid community. His buddy and bodyguard Knuckles said so. Knuckles was a big-shouldered bruiser who became Knuckles by using his knuckles to relieve drunks of their belligerence. "When Goblin spoke," Knuckles said, "people listened." Back in New Orleans, Louisiana, back in NOLA, Goblin prowled the French Quarter, a world of its own along the Mississippi, its heart beating to Bourbon Street's jazz, where everyone knew everyone's business, who slept with whom, who had warrants out, who was most likely to OD. There the Scurvy Bastards called him "Admiral." I, the grandfather, had known him as Jared, a shy kid, always fun but always in the background. Not so in NOLA, not after years on the road. By the time he returned from Myrtle Beach, he had grown into the boss. He was Goblin, who made things happen.

He made a kid feel welcome. A kid named Eddo, seventeen years old, told me the story:

I was new to NOLA, and I ended up getting blacked out on Bourbon Street and woke up on the sidewalk. I had no idea where I was, where my friends were, or where my gear was. I was fucked. Oh, and to top it off, I was DT"ing. Not a fun combination. I wandered around the Quarter and eventually bumped into Goblin sitting with a girl named Alex Tallent.

He took me under his wing. He told me to sit down with them and wait. We sat and drank. Eventually, my friends found me. Most kids who frequent NOLA are pretty pretentious, so it was surprising that Goblin offered to let me hang out with him and wait. It was really cool. I was lost in a city I had never been to, and fresh as fuck. That combination can be really dangerous in New Orleans, which is a pretty dangerous place anyway. Goblin was always like that, though. Always willing to help out another traveler. The Scurvy code: "Help is always on the way!"

ooooo

Always bringing help, Goblin also did a mass baptism. Austin Hall, a kid with a guitar, had hitchhiked three days from Illinois. He heard somebody on Bourbon Street shout, "'Oy! Come here, you! Welcome, we're going to have some fun,'" Hall said. "He brought that cane with him on the bus from Myrtle Beach, and he marched down the street like a damned drum major. Dude, one time we led a bunch of tourists down to the Mississippi. Goblin had this weird hat on and told 'em he was an itinerant preacher who'd baptize them in the river. Fuckin' gross river water. They asked if they could just dip their feet in it, and Goblin said, 'No, the Lord says I gotta pour it over your head,' and they let him do it—about fifteen of 'em."

He created a wedding. He knew the bride, Sarafina Scarlet. She played a guitar and sang on Christine Maynard's doorstep by the Decatur Street daiquiri shop. Her face had been on the side of a milk carton because she had run away from a girls' home in California. Sarafina carried her guitar across her back to the boardwalk by the Mississippi, to Checkpoint Charlie's, to her squat in the Eighth Ward. Christine said, "Sarafina had a delicate, lilting voice with a baseline of grit and determination."

Jared knew her and might have loved her because he made it his business to know all the pretty ones, and if it's true that we fall in love with another version of ourselves, Sarafina was that, a doll given life, her face soft and golden. What they had together was something other than a romantic relationship, maybe something better.

She said, "Goblin and I never so much as kissed, though the connection we had was very strong. It was more that we just understood each other. He was one of the most kindhearted kids I ever met on the road. Not a bad attitude or one to cause trouble. He just loved to be around friends and have a good time and be sweet to people. He always greeted me with the biggest hug, and we always laughed together. Even after he got hit by the car, he hobbled around with a cane looking for the next adventure with all our friends. I gave him the nickname 'Hobblin' Goblin.' If he had feelings for me, he never did anything about them. I was dating another boy at the time."

That boy was Patrizio, tall, dark, and exotic. So Jared rounded up people for a Sarafina-Patrizio wedding, set for seven o'clock in Jackson Square, on the walkway in front of St. Louis Cathedral.

For a wedding, he wanted music. He enlisted the Illinois kid, Hall. They'd made some money on the street, Hall with the guitar, Jared singing along on "Wayfaring Stranger."

> *I'm just a poor wayfaring stranger*
> *Traveling through this world below*
> *There is no sickness, no toil, nor danger*
> *In that bright land to which I go*

And Jared remembered, from Halloween night on the wharf, the girl with the mandolin, the girl traveling with Lyndzy.

"Put the word out," he said at the gathering. "I want Maggie and her green mandolin."

That afternoon Maggie came to the cathedral. Goblin took her in his arms and they danced, and soon enough he didn't care if she played the mandolin at all. Stray had been right when she said, Forget the runaway in San Diego, you'll find better in New Orleans. The better was Maggie. There would be others, and they would come along soon, but Maggie was the one. They danced that night, and she said she was leaving NOLA the next day and they ought to meet up again sometime somewhere.

All the Scurvy Bastards who could get upright came to the wedding. The ceremony's officiant was a dandy dressed in all whites, and from a distance he seemed to be wearing a fine tuxedo. Up close, the whites turned out to be a line cook's shirt and apron.

Christine Maynard attended the festivities in her roles as a chronicler of the street kids' lives and, more important to her, as a caring, protective presence. She had nearly been killed in an automobile accident years before. For her, life ever after had been an adventure, the more daring the better. She came with an earth mother–goddess–warrior–princess gonna-save-the-world vibe. She saw in the street kids a freedom so beautiful as to be seductive and so seductive as to hide its dangers. She made her home their home when they needed it. Both Sarafina and Patrizio had stayed there, and then the trouble named Puzzles came to live with her, and in a time of need, Jared too would crash at Christine's.

The day of the wedding, Christine knew Jared only as Puzzles's friend, another of the travelin' kids she saw now and then. In her photographs made at Jackson Square, Jared looked a weary mess. Doctors in Myrtle Beach had given him permission to travel, but those doctors may have thought of travel as something done in comfort, not on a bouncing Greyhound. Jared was three months removed from a near-death experience and only two weeks before had taken his mother's mile-on-the-beach test. Still, in every Maynard photograph, with a walking stick in hand, a weary mess or not, the Admiral was in charge and laughing.

Jared had created his preferred life, a wanderer's life, at home nowhere and everywhere. He had chosen to live on the streets of the nation's capital and then wherever the winds of whim took him. By saying no to a lawsuit that might have won him $600,000, he passed on a chance to get out of a life with dangers more subtle and just as deadly as an automobile appearing from nowhere.

His first week back in New Orleans, I called and said what everyone who ever loved an addict has said: "I love you, Jared, but you gotta quit it. Quit the drinking. You gotta take care of yourself."

He said what every addict ever has said: "I will, Grandpa, I will, don't worry about me."

He was lying, and we both knew it. His words were designed to let me know only that he heard my voice. He knew that if he told me, after a few minutes, "Don't worry about me," I would understand the conversation was over.

ooooo

What Jared did too much of on the road was drink, and what he did too often was fall into fights with guys who beat the shit out of him. His original urban-survival mentor in Virginia, Michael Stephen, said that Jared, though small and thin, could "seriously fuck you up if you messed with his friends." But this ability came with a flaw. "He was not the smartest guy about it. He would fight really big dudes."

The morning of May 15, 2011, Lynn called with the results of one of those encounters.

"Jared's back in the hospital," she said.

He had been gone from Myrtle Beach for seventy-three days.

"He got slugged in the face last night, fell, and hit his head on a flagstone," she said. "There's bleeding in the brain. The doctor said he's 'serious but stable.' Then a nurse came on and asked if anyone had power of attorney for Jared. I said, 'Why do you want to know that?' She said, 'It's a life-and-death issue, and we need to know what to do.' I told her, 'Just fix my child. Whatever you need to do, fix my child.'"

A son facing a "life-and-death issue" should have caused a mother and a father, or even a grandfather invested in a boy's well-being, to go to New Orleans. Why we didn't go, I don't know, other than it seemed that being beaten was not as serious as being run down by a car. In thinking that we didn't need to go to New Orleans, we could not have been more mistaken. Read these hospital reports and weep:

TULANE MEDICAL CENTER
Name: Kindred, Jared
DOB: 12/08/88
Admit Date: 05/15/11

History: This is a 22-year-old male who presents after being "beaten up." The patient arrives by EMS. He states he was in a fight and he got "bleeped" up. He states he was not hit with anything other than a fist. He states he was not knocked out. He did get knocked to the ground on a couple of occasions. The patient admits to alcohol intake tonight. Denies any drug use tonight . . .

On discharge May 26:

ADMITTING HISTORY AND PHYSICAL

Mr. Kindred was admitted to the intensive care unit after being assaulted and having bilateral frontal contusions. He is a well-known alcoholic. He did extremely well despite alcohol withdrawal. He was put on Ativan drip for treatment of delirium tremens with vitamin B12 every day. Mr. Kindred wanted to leave against medical advice initially, and psychiatry restricted him to hospital. The patient had no further complications and his behavior came under control. He did not have neurological deficits. CT scan of his head showed contusions were more than 95 percent resolved without any mass effect.

The patient's behavior was much better, and he stated several times that he was wanting to go to Baton Rouge, to decrease his drinking behavior.

Discharge Instructions: No driving, no weightlifting, no sports activities, no drinking for at least two weeks. The patient was told that he will put his life at risk if he were to resume his drinking behavior.

His was a life of risk. Trains. Beatings. Vodka. If he could do something about the first two, there was little he could do about the alcohol addiction. He could nod to doctors and say what was expected of him, that, yes, he planned to go to Baton Rouge and cut down on the drinking. But a week after he left the hospital, Jared was not in Baton Rouge. He was hobbling, with his walking stick in hand, along Decatur Street in the boiling heat of a New Orleans summer's-coming day.

"Yes, somebody hit him, and his head hit a rock down by the Mississippi where his crowd would congregate and drink," Christine Maynard said. "Probably stupid drunk stuff. A few times every year, a ton of really dangerous street people, grown men and women, show up. There are knifings, and these people get in your face and demand money. They're scary. He was wobbly and still dizzy from the head injury and looked horrible. I asked him to come to my house, but he was a little drunk and guys on the street teased him. He kept saying something like, 'Houses are for pussies, and I'm not going in any house.'"

Puzzles, who was on the street with Maynard looking for the friend he called "my little brother," wrapped an arm around Jared, lifted him, pulled him close, and half-carried him through that red door at 907 Decatur Street and up the stairs to Maynard's apartment. Puzzles dropped Jared on a fancy leather couch from which he seldom stirred for the next five days.

Christine's Story

In those five days, Jared made a remarkable turnaround. Nourishment, some cleaning up, lots of sleep. He was living on a very comfortable couch and was cared for and loved on and listened to. It was a sacred space, and I didn't understand why at the time. I didn't question. It was what it was supposed to be.

And then he wasn't sleeping all the time anymore. His color was better. That's when he started talking.

The talking—that's when I realized how much he loved life. His stories were kaleidoscopic and filled with minutiae, and he was gulping down experiences. Nothing was lost on him. Everything he said showed his love of people and the dizzying possibilities and never, never wanting to slow down. Never wanting the kaleidoscope to stop turning. He wanted life to be burning jewels all lit up forever.

About 8:00 a.m. every day, he'd wake up and go to the bathroom, where he'd throw up, or have the dry heaves, and then he'd feel better. He'd say, "I just need a little vodka and I'll be all right." I'd buy him a half-pint of Taaka, maybe a pint, it was $9. He'd have just a little bit, and then I'd make him eat the omelets Puzzles made, goat cheese and other delicacies—really eat, as with the fork actually going into his mouth. Puzzles would say, "Little baby Goblin getting fed." And Goblin would say, "Fuck you, Puzzles." And they'd be laughing.

I spoke a lot about his future possibilities for a sustainable life. He wanted to work with his hands. I wanted him to write stories about his traveling adventures and the life. He was light and funny and kind and easy to please and special. I loved him very much.

He talked about his childhood in amazing detail. He seemed to remember everything, what the setting was, the hills, trees, what one person said and what the other person said, and what the weather was. He told me about riding a bike in his neighborhood and how much he liked the feeling of the wind—like, I imagine, the wind he felt on trains.

In those times, he was my glorious Peter Pan. He had created a world he loved and never wanted to leave. That other world can be so cold and cruel. He wanted a place where he could be himself and not what somebody thought he should be. That other world—he said you had to have a job and a car and a house or else people thought you were worthless. We need more kids brave enough to tell that other world, "I don't need you, I can be happy without you." We need more Goblins, not fewer.

ooooo

Eclectic in her collection of passions, Christine had a soft spot for men who beat up each other for a living, a crowd of young prize-fighters that she had photographed in a New Orleans boxing gym. "When Jared found that out," she said, "he quite excitedly told me that I ought to talk to his grandpa about Muhammad Ali."

I met Ali in 1966, covered ten of his heavyweight champion-ship fights, and in 2006 wrote a dual biography of Ali and Howard Cosell. Best of all were the bedtime stories I told the boy about another boy, Cassius Marcellus Clay Jr., who grew up to be Ali.

In the summer of 2011, Jared called and said, "Christine wants to see that picture of you and Muhammad." In that photograph, I held a notebook and watched Ali warm up for a fight. I texted it to Jared. Three years later, after everything that would happen, I looked through the messages on his phone. He had kept the picture.

ooooo

I'd look at his vodka bottle and by 11:00 a.m., before we'd gone out-side, he would have had just two ounces of vodka, estimating. I was no expert, but my understanding was that the DTs could kill him and he had to keep a little bit of alcohol in his system. I did make him eat, those baby-bird bites. He began to wash up a little bit, which caused Puz-zles to remark that he hadn't seen that before. Cleaned up, Goblin was pretty, with lovely, delicate features and so fair and blue-eyed. The girls all loved him.

His manners were perfect. If someone knocked on the door and I was indisposed, he'd answer the door, introduce himself, and ask the person to wait, she'll be right here. He was so polite. He loved people. With-out the blue tattoo on his face and the dirt everywhere, he could have been anything. Fraternity president, campus leader, organizer of a cause group—anything. He was just so darn upbeat with an infectious enthusiasm for whatever was going on.

We talked, too, about the train-hopping. He did it both for the fun and to get somewhere. He loved it. There was the secret hoboes-only white book [the "Crew Change Guide"] of what each train route was like, friendly or not, where to stash your pack, everything you needed to know to hop out. There was the anticipation of going on a vacation, what food and drink and what to bring to burn for heat. The fear of the "bulls" catching you. The uber-coolness of it all. The scenery, the challenges, the caring for others, the hiding from bulls.

Getting ready for the trains was as much of a drug for Goblin as the actual hopping. There was danger, and he knew it. Sarafina Scarlet was dragged by a train and lived—her leg got hung up and she didn't make the jump into the moving car, and finally her leg came loose and she got lucky, she didn't fall under the train. And the other dangers: drugs, alcohol, hepatitis infections, and bad people KO'ing you. The danger seems to me something to balance how the kids romanticize the hoppin' hobo life.

After Goblin left my apartment and rejoined the revelers on the street, anytime he saw me, he would wave so big and run a few steps and have to hop and hobble. I'd run toward him, and he'd hug me like he hadn't seen me in twenty years. If there was a new addition to the kids, he'd introduce me. "This is her, this is Christine, she's the lady I told you about."

He brought joy. He was graced with beauty, almost a feminine beauty, with a symmetry of lips, nose, eyes. As the summer went on, his coloring changed from glowing golden brown to rosy. And he had a strong musculature, no weakling, like a bantam rooster.

My hobblin' Goblin. He made my heart light with laughter and love.

SEVEN

Stories grow slowly. A detail here, a memory there. Looking for something else, the storyteller finds a photograph, a document, lines from a forgotten journal. More often than he cares to admit, he doesn't at first see what's there to be seen. He sees it only later when he has told parts of the story so often that he finally hears how those parts connect. It was late in this story when I realized that Jared's troubled times on the road overlapped my mother's last days in a nursing home. So I should tell her story.

My father built a little white two-story house by the Illinois Central Railroad tracks. When I say "by the tracks," I mean our house was separated from the tracks only by a dirt road. My bedroom was upstairs. I climbed through a window onto the porch roof, and with a Boy Scout telescope in my rear pocket and my knees and elbows scratching against grainy shingles, I scooched up the steep roof and leaned against the chimney and through my looking glass searched for distant places. I wanted to know what was out there. I could see McLean, a village three miles north. My hometown, Atlanta, Illinois, population 1,600, sits along the famous US Route 66, which ran on the other side of our railroad tracks. The 10:10 Illinois Central caused my bedroom to tremble. Sometimes I dreamed I was Superman, faster than a speeding locomotive. At night, trains passing our house would shake my bed with their sudden thunder. The train would be at my window and then gone, moving in the darkness. I could hear its whistle at the depot crossing just before it left the city limits heading to destinations unknown to me. Dad said the trains came our way from Chicago.

"Where's Chicago?" I said.

He said, "The Cubs play there."

I thought it would be fun to swing up into a boxcar, the way cowboys did in movies. It wasn't that I wanted to go to Chicago, wherever that was. I just wanted to be someplace else, a place far away, even farther away than my telescope could take me. Long before Jared, I wanted to be Jared.

During the day, trains stopped at the depot in Atlanta. From boxcars at the back of the string, men would jump out. In the 1940s, the hoboes knew if they hustled down the ballast and across that dirt road to that little white two-story house with the apple trees in the backyard, a lovely woman would have cheese sandwiches ready, wrapped in waxed paper or, if she had run out of paper, wrapped in pieces of the bread sack itself. Before they left, the woman would hand the men brown paper bags to carry apples back to the train. Maybe it happened that way everywhere along the Illinois Central route. I prefer to think that only my mother was so lovely as to care that hoboes had something to eat while they rode the rails in search of a day's work.

Some of this I remembered. Some of it my mother told me one day in May of 2011—a day when Jared had been taken to a New

Orleans hospital, where he was reported to be in "serious but stable" condition after a head injury incurred in a street fight.

Mom was ninety-four years old and living in a nursing home in Morton, Illinois. After forty-five years away, Cheryl and I had come home. To say the decision to move from Virginia to Illinois puzzled our friends is to understate the pity they held for us. Gene Weingarten, a two-time Pulitzer winner for the *Washington Post*, said, "To Chicago, America, I hope, not some stinkweed hamlet." Even our New Zealand–born horse veterinarian wondered why anyone would voluntarily exchange the rich, verdant landscapes of Virginia for the arctic/tropic weather of a bankrupt flyover state whose governors made a habit of winding up in prison. She said, "What did you do wrong?"

Each of our previous moves—from Illinois to Kentucky to Washington, DC, to Georgia to Virginia—had been made for a job. This move was for better reasons. Mom was failing, and I felt a tug of the heart to be near her. My sister, Sandra, was there with a wonderful extended family of children, grandchildren, and great-grandchildren. It was time to close the circle. My father had died forty-eight years before, only fifty-one years old. When it was Mom's time, I wanted to be there.

She was tough and smart. For years she said, "I'm a survivor," and she proved it daily. She had come of age during the Depression and believed that work was the answer to every question. In the 1950s at the Dixie Truckers Stop in McLean—I could see its roof from our roof—when no one else would serve dinner to African Americans, Mom waited tables for Louis Armstrong and his jazz band driving from St. Louis to Chicago on Route 66. "Louis left a $5 tip and said be sure to be at work next week because he'd be coming through the other direction," Mom said. Twenty-five years later, at a state institution for the developmentally challenged, she did a heroine's work with children and adults who needed a heroine every day. She called them "my kids."

A month before I sat with her in the nursing home, a doctor had pronounced her all but dead. She had the flu or pneumonia or a bad cold, something that left her weak. In two days in a hospital, she had become cadaverous, her face locked in the rictus look of death. I asked the doctor, "What's going on? She wasn't this bad when she came in." Whatever the doctor said, I remember only four words: " . . . the end of life."

Somehow Mom left that hospital and moved into the Apostolic Christian Restmor nursing home. She had lived with Sandy the previous eight years, and we had dreaded the idea of a nursing home. Mom was assigned to a room with a woman she had never met, Lena Vignieri, age ninety-six. Lena, too, had been so weak during a stay in a hospital as to be seen as near death.

Happily, Mom and Lena exceeded all expectations. In a picture taken with a Mother's Day coming, the nonagenarians, both wearing happy red hats, were caught in a fit of laughter. Mom is on the left—Marie Magdalena Maloney Kindred Cheek. Her eyes are squeezed shut by whatever happy thought has lit her up. On the right is Lena Scardello Vignieri. Standing behind them are their daughters, Sandy Litwiller and Rose Mary Detweiler.

On April 12, 2011, we thought Mom would soon be dead. Sixteen days later, at Restmor, she walked on her own for five minutes. She was not at the end of life—she was at a new beginning. For no reason other than it's what reporters do, I made notes of Mom's comeback in the nursing home:

Mom now says she's rolling around Restmor so much that "they're always looking for me!" She moves the wheelchair with her

feet. "I can do anything in this wheelchair that anybody else
can do!" Voice no longer squeaky.
A therapist checked Mom's ability to chew her food and swallow.
The therapist asked, "Can you cough for me?" Mom's hearing,
never good, wasn't good this day either. "Oh, sure! I talk all
the time!"
Mom says Dad "never went to a dentist or doctor. He said God
made him this way, he'd stay that way. Poor guy."
"Gotta go where life leads you." Made a motion with her hand,
like a fish swimming in a stream. "Wherever."
"Age is nothing, life's what's important."
"I'm still here, believe it or not!"

Mom and Lena were hardscrabble tough. Both were daughters
of coal miners. Mom worked in her mother's tavern. Lena and her
husband operated a tavern. Both women had lived lives they could
not have imagined. They passed through the Depression. They
survived World Wars I and II. They saw a man walk on the moon.
Together, they gave birth to four children who gave them sixteen
grandchildren, thirty-two great-grandchildren, and two great-
great grandchildren.

Neither woman could hear anything much under a shout. Mom
refused hearing aids; she believed it wasn't her problem ("People
just need to speak up!"). Lena wore hearing aids but only occasionally thought to turn them on. Yet magically, they seemed to know
what each other said. They communicated through a spiritual te-
lepathy of winks and whispers, giggles and smiles, hand-holdings
and kisses on the forehead. No one understood how it was done, or
what caused it to be done, and we didn't much care as we watched
in wonder while these two frail, dying women gave each other

strength. Lena made Mom laugh. And Mom saw it as her job to take care of Lena and be a heroine for all those really old people in the place, some of them older than her but none so old that they weren't her "kids" needing her.

At dinner that evening in the nursing home, she told a woman, "You gotta find a way to eat, you can't just look at your food."

Mom demonstrated. "Like this." With her right hand, she dipped a spoon into a bowl of creamed corn. Then she reached over with her left hand to grasp her right wrist. With the left hand, she lifted her right arm to bring the spoonful of corn to her mouth.

"See?" she said.

Mom's years at Restmor were life-affirming. She laughed one day as she said, "Everybody asks me how old I am, and I don't know." Then she smacked her forehead. "I don't have an area in my brain for that." She knew the question was not about her age but her expiration date. "When I'm old enough to die," she said, and she said it forcefully, "I'll die."

She saw no reason to worry. She knew how to handle it. Until she was old enough to die, by damn she would live. For some, death comes on the dark wings of silence, fear, and sorrow. Not for Mom. In her dying, she would laugh and show her kids how to eat their corn.

I wasn't sure she remembered her great-grandson Jared. She had seen him only once, as a toddler. On May 15, 2011, I told her that he was in a hospital in New Orleans.

"What's he doing down there?" Mom asked.

"He's living on the road now," I said. "He's what they call a train-hopper."

Mom raised up in her wheelchair and said, "You mean, like a hobo?" Then she told the cheese sandwich story.

Some coincidences defy explanation. Failing an explanation, someone long ago said, "Coincidence is God's way of working anonymously." If that's so—and why not?—my conversation with Mom had taken us into coincidence territory. Maybe because I wanted it to be so, or maybe because it was so, I decided Mom's story connected us all. Dad built our house along railroad tracks that reached New Orleans. She made cheese sandwiches for hoboes. I shinnied up to a rooftop because I was wired with a wanderer's instinct. Trains rocked me to sleep as they would rock Jared to sleep. They promised to take us away from where we were to where we'd rather be, if only we knew where that place was.

EIGHT

Jared stayed at Christine's a month before again answering the call for movement. By then, Puzzles was in jail for having leaped into the Mississippi for a morning swim. Christine wrote, "When Puzzles created chaos, he invoked Deities of fucking up. Trickster spirits, Bacchanalian excess, take no prisoners. He had public drunkenness and disturbing the peace attachments punctuating the map of America. At a gay bar he frequented, Corner Pocket, an old man, shook his head when he saw me with Puzzles, smiled, and said, 'He's a bad, bad boy.'"

Out of jail, that bad boy gathered up the hobblin' Goblin for a road trip. They hitched a ride to New York City, and Jared spent the summer of 2011 sleeping in a gazebo on the Coney Island boardwalk. There was a girl. Of course a girl, another girl, always a girl with Goblin, Goblin looking for love as if he'd never known love. She was tall, dark, and beautiful, Puerto Rican–French, nineteen years old. She called herself Solzy Twitch Leboy. Those words sounded so beautiful I never asked why she was called that. I didn't care. It added to the mystery of a girl Goblin knew well when knowing girls well made him feel good.

She had done a year of college before a drug habit ended that. "Instead of moving back home," she said, "I got really drunk and curled up on the sidewalk out front of a Kmart on Astor Place." From then on, she lived on the street. She was in Manhattan when she met two travelin' kids up from New Orleans, Goblin and Puzzles.

"Goblin asked me if I wanted to go to Coney Island with them," Solzy said. "I said yes because I thought he was hot." She also provided a new viewpoint on the facial tattoo that had caused his mother grief. "He was pretty awesome and definitely a flirt. He talked to every girl who passed by. I loved his eyes and his smile and that sick face tat. He was also hilarious. He always had people laughing. He wasn't afraid to sing songs that others in the group might make fun of him for. He did some silly Blink-182 songs for me. He wasn't afraid to dance, make funny faces, and do silly voices. He had a happy essence about him."

Because she had at least a fraction of interest in what went on around her and knew she might want to know what she was like in those long-ago Coney Island days, Solzy bought a journal. When she had something to say, she wrote it down there, like this about the Jared/Goblin boy: "Our first night together, we made love in a playground in the sand. He mentioned a pain in his lower abs"—this was nine months after the surgeries in Arizona—"and I noticed a huge scar right below his belly button. I kissed it gently. We've been together every moment since then."

The gazebo was home. Tourists stopped by to take pictures of the sleeping beauties, not just Jared and Solzy but sometimes as many as a dozen kids piled in there. It had the look of a flea market, filled with stuff hanging from the edges, artifacts picked up around the island and carried home as memorials to an era. Solzy said, "We 'decorated' in a drunken state with whatever we could find," which is how a painted carousel horse came to hang from the gazebo eaves.

Late one night, it seemed a good idea to break into Luna Park, one of the island's three amusement parks.

"As we walked along the boardwalk," Solzy said, "we weren't particularly looking for a way in when we spotted a small fence that appeared easy to climb over."

Puzzles and his girlfriend, Kaitlin, were accomplices. "Puzzles was our tallest, so he made it over, no problem. Goblin and I laughed as Kaitlin tried to join him, but she was too drunk to make it more than two feet off the ground."

Once Solzy was in the park, she asked Jared to hop over the fence. He was still the hobblin' Goblin, so . . .

"He looked at me like I was crazy, shook his head no, and laughed that beautiful laugh of his. So Puzzles and I examined this ride that goes in circles really fast with music blasting. I climbed over the barriers and into one of the cars and waited for Puzzles to figure out how to turn it on."

Then she heard Goblin.

"How you guys going to get off that thing?" he said. Adding, "Puzzles, you ever hopped off a train going as fast as this shit will once it's turned on?"

With the decision put in terms a train-hopper understood, Puzzles chose discretion, and the crew returned to the gazebo, safe from self-harm for the moment and laughing at the things kids will do under the influence of whatever substance they were into at the moment.

SOLZY'S STORY

Goblin wasn't one of those guys that you had to be afraid of. He was a drunk you could have fun with. He was relaxed, he wasn't afraid to be who he was. Like the way he walked. He still had the limp from his accident, and he wore these pants that were too big. So he'd be limping along, his pants falling down, him pulling 'em up. It was funny and charming.

There were a lot of layers to him. We had a really deep conversation about children. He supposedly almost had a child in New Orleans—at least that's what he heard, though I don't think he believed it. One thing I admired, he was an addict who didn't put his substance above you. He was a big drinker. Alcohol, alcohol, alcohol. He wanted his vodka. Vodka, his poison of choice. But he never put the substance above friends. Not many addicts would do that.

We were both drinking all the time. We were both sick and didn't know it. Kaitlin, my best friend, told me, "You guys are sleeping way too much," and I thought, Nothing else I want to do, just drink and sleep. A lot of people confuse that behavior, sleeping so much, with using heroin. In our time together, I know Jared never did drugs, not at all, he was all alcohol all the time.

That's the thing, you're an addict and you think you're in control. Drinking, I was queen of the world. You think you're in control, but the drug is taking control of you. You're living for the next drink.

Jared would wake up, vomit, usually some blood, feel like crap, and go make money to go to the liquor store for the next bottle. I never heard him say he wanted to stop. He just didn't really care. It's what made him happy.

I said you didn't have to be afraid of Goblin, and that was true, he was sweet, but like all of us he had his moments, like the day the shit really hit the fan with him and Kaitlin.

They'd been at each other's throats on and off since we got together. Kaitlin could be a little much to handle. Puzzles and I went for a walk and on the way back we heard Goblin and Kaitlin yelling. He was calling her annoying, and she threatened to punch him, after which Goblin charged at her and I jumped in front of him.

I told him to calm the fuck down and that he knew better than to put his hands on her. It took him a couple minutes, but he finally seemed like he wasn't going to knock her lights out. Kaitlin and I left for the other side of the boardwalk.

The next morning, Goblin looked so sad. He gave me a hug and told me he missed me. I wanted to melt in his arms and just have him hold me. But I stood strong. As beautiful and as charming as he is, he almost hit a girl.

Then, the morning after that, I woke up with horribly scraped knees. I don't remember anything. Kaitlin told me that Goblin and I got into it and other people got involved. But I guess everything turned out okay because we were all back together in our cozy little gazebo and Goblin was curled up, snoring quietly, next to me.

And the hurricane—Hurricane Irene hit Brooklyn the twenty-ninth of August 2011. Everyone had ditched us. The wind was heavy, and Goblin hated the rain, so he'd been bitching since Kaitlin tried to wake us up. I was too drunk and too tired to speak to her, so I just nuzzled into Goblin's chest and continued sleeping until finally they moved us all off Coney Island and gave us a free train ride into the city.

We weren't going to stay in some homeless shelter, but holy shit, that night was out of control. So many people, about fifteen of us from Coney Island, all sleeping on the steps to this apartment building on Second Avenue. In addition, there were about twenty hippie punks sleeping on top of each other, with three dogs, and everybody trying to stay out of the two inches of water that flowed below the second step.

It's not the life for everybody, I know that. But I loved it. There's nothing more freeing. The world was my home. And at the same time there's nothing more mentally trying. It's constant chaos. I got to where I wasn't suicidal, but I didn't care if I lived or died. So I got out of that life.

Goblin was a soul that was meant to just keep going.

Our time ended one day when he just said he had to go back to New Orleans. I saw him in New York sometime later. I didn't say hi or anything. By that point, I was with my current fiancé, and Goblin was walking around downtown with two girls on his arms. I had to laugh, the cute little flirt.

⋮ NINE ⋮

As fraternal twins, Jared and Jacob looked enough alike to be brothers, both blond, blue-eyed, small, slight. But there was no mistaking which brother was which. The sweetheart Jared came with a baby's face, open, round, soft; Jacob's was a closed fist, giving away nothing, hard, with eyes full of suspicion. Jared's default look was a smile, Jacob's a scowl. Jared invited you in, Jacob closed you out. Jacob had stumbled through the mindless work of handyman jobs and flipping burgers. Jared earned $194.18 his first week at a Ben & Jerry's ice cream shop before being fired for spiking his own milkshake with vodka. After high school, the brothers never again lived together.

Jared found Michael Stephen in his Alexandria squat and then, under the influence of bottom-shelf vodka, wandered across the map never much caring where the trains stopped as long as they took him someplace different each time. Jacob lasted one semester at a community college. Then he floated between our place in Virginia and an uncle's in California and a friend's in Pennsylvania.

He worked in a pool hall and he worked in a bar. He was paid in tip money and drinks, occasionally picking up a few dollars in nine-ball games. At twenty-two, it was his way of joining his lost brother. We wondered if they could ever find their way into the light.

I knew only that they rooted for each other.

Late in 2011, shortly after Jared left Coney Island, Jacob's wanderings brought him to his mother's doorstep in Myrtle Beach. He arrived with an unusual touch of ambition. He wanted to go to school. He thought it would be neat to be an audio engineer. But Lynn had just learned about the Pittsburgh Institute of Aeronautics, a school that trained aviation mechanics. PIA was about to open a Myrtle Beach branch a half-hour from her house.

Jacob liked the idea. He fancied himself a master of machines. He had done auto mechanic's work alongside his dad and had rebuilt a twenty-year-old BMW coupe and driven it another ten years. For Jacob, the aeronautics school's selling point was its report that graduates of its two-year program could count on landing a job with a starting salary between $40,000 and $60,000. Jacob had a girlfriend in Virginia. The promise of that kind of money suggested marriage, a home, and a family.

Jared, for one, was impressed. When Jacob announced his plan to become a Federal Aviation Administration–certified mechanic, Jared said, "Wow! Then you can get a big-ass house and have a room for me and rooms for our friends."

Jacob understood that fraternal twins were no more alike than brothers born in different years, but he saw enough curious connections that he never totally bought into that idea of separateness. "I'd get into trouble at school," Jacob said. "Like, the teacher would have us write what we did over the weekend and I'd always write,

'We hung out, we walked in the woods, we went fishing.' It was always 'we' instead of 'I.' Because we did everything together."

He met a homeless man at a gas station. "I talked to him, gave him some change, told him my name was Jacob. We talked some a long time and finally I left, and when I was leaving, he said, 'Thanks, Jared.' What? Jared? I'd never mentioned Jared. A lot of people with no clue I even had a brother would meet me and call me Jared. What's that about?"

At recess in kindergarten, Jacob saw Jared swinging on monkey bars until, halfway across, he stopped. Here came a kid from the other direction, a second grader, a bigger kid. The kid kicked Jared in the chest, knocking him off the bars and to the ground, where he broke an arm.

"I was afraid of heights back then," Jacob said, "but the first thing I did was run and jump on the monkey bars and swing across to that kid and I kicked *him* in the chest and knocked him off. Then I jumped off and landed right on top of him and proceeded to punch him in the face, and I would not stop punching him. Teachers had to pull me off of him. I don't remember this, but Mom says I beat the shit out of the kid so bad that it took five minutes to wash the blood off of him before they could figure out who he was."

It was brotherly love in the way that things happen with brothers. "Yeah, we'd be at each other a lot. You know that story where I hung Jared over the railing by his ankles?"

"Do tell," I said. "I've heard a version of it."

By Jacob's account, the boys-will-be-boys thing started in his bedroom upstairs, moved onto the loft landing, and continued until he hoisted Jared over the railing, dangling in midair, upside down, his head six feet from the living room floor. It was high enough—higher than monkey bars—that a kid dropped from there might get hurt in ways the other kid didn't intend.

"Dad and Lisa were freaking out, like, what was happening, what could they do? Hell, I wasn't going to drop him," Jacob said. "Anyway, Dad was about right below us. He'd have caught him."

That was the summer that Jeff and Lisa split up the boys. They sent Jared to live with his mother eighty miles away. That was the summer of the phone call I got while on a vacation trip in Montana, the summer Jeff told me about the boys fighting and the loft railing incident, the summer he said, "*I'm the parent here.*"

Jacob said, "Yeah, that's the story, that they made Jared move to Mom's so we wouldn't fight and do all that shit—and that's total bullshit. The whole reason was because Lisa was scared Kaleb would somehow get hurt and she didn't want Jared there. The last straw was Jared didn't want to go to school one day, and Lisa was telling him he had to go to school, and he said, 'No, I'm not going, I'm going to stay here.' And Lisa couldn't get him up out of bed and get him to school, and she's like, 'Okay, I'm done with you, you stay here today. I'm done with you, you're going to go live with your mom after this.' And that weekend was the weekend he went to live with Mom."

Jacob said he had a choice. He could go with Jared or stay in Locust Grove. "I felt really bad that Jared was going there and I wasn't. But we did see each other every other weekend, back and forth between Mom's and Dad's. It was just one more thing that was screwed up. Our whole life it was, like, Georgia, Virginia, Alexandria, Fairfax, Locust Grove—why the hell can't we stay in one spot? We'd be in one school and make friends, the next year we'd be out. So I wanted to stay in Locust Grove."

Through it all, he said, there was one constant: they were brothers. "In the big picture, whether we lived together every day

or not, it didn't matter. Because when anything got to be important, we always had each other."

And yet . . .

Jacob told me a story.

One morning in his first year at the Myrtle Beach aviation-
mechanic school, he stopped at the refrigerator to grab a breakfast taco. Only it was gone and he shouted out, "Jared, you eat my
taco?"

"Yeah, I was hungry."

"Fuck that. Get your own tacos."

Jared and Lyndzy had come to Myrtle Beach for a weeklong
stop that left Jacob bewildered by what he saw in their behavior.

"They didn't want to go anywhere or do anything, they just sat
in the house, played video games, and drank," Jacob said. "Sometimes while I was out going to school, they'd go panhandle to get
some giant bottle of vodka. They were just drunk the whole week,
never really sober."

"What'd you think of it?" I said.

"I wasn't a fan of it, and Jared knew it."

"Did you talk to him about it?"

"Yeah, and he said, 'I can't help it, man. If I stop, I'll get the
shakes and I'll start seizing. I have to drink.' I said, 'Well, slowly
bring yourself down off of it. Don't get drunk whenever you drink.
Just drink to get well. Try to get yourself to come down off of it.'"

A pause here.

"But he wouldn't," Jacob said. "He didn't listen to anybody. He
wasn't listening to me. He wasn't listening to Mom. He did what
he wanted to. They slept in my living room on an air mattress, and
he'd wake up in the middle of the night because he'd start DT'ing.
They slept with a bottle of vodka next to the bed. He'd take a couple swigs off it, then lay there, and go back to sleep."

Maybe only a brother could know what Jacob then knew. Maybe you had to have lived in the womb with Jared. Maybe you had to protect him from monkey-bars bullies to know it. If you shared every day of your life to age eleven and then, separated by order of your parents, met every weekend at one parent's or the other's, maybe then you could feel what Jacob said he felt that week in Myrtle Beach. Maybe you had to know, by your own failings, the trouble that came with alcohol.

Jacob said, "What I felt about Jared, it's an instinct thing, a gut feeling. He's gone."

I said, "What do you mean, 'gone'?"

His answer was chilling.

"That whole week in Myrtle Beach," Jacob said, "I liked being able to see him and everything. But when it got to that point where he had to drink, he wasn't Jared anymore. He was something else in the shell of Jared. Every now and then you'd get a glimpse. But mostly it was whatever the hell it was nestled in the shell of Jared. It looked like Jared, talked like Jared, but it wasn't Jared."

TEN

Goblin's life is the story, and I am his grandfather telling it. So there is love in the telling. And yet, when the grandfather is also a reporter moving into a world unknown, he needs good reason to think the story is real and true. He started the reporting with only a name. Goblin's mother knew a name of a girl on Goblin's first train ride. "Stray," the mother said. A Facebook search turned up a Stray Falldowngoboom. By Stray's stories, the grandfather moved through the New Mexico night on a thundering freight with the dancing boy. Maybe Jared danced, maybe he didn't, but the story is the truth as his road dogs remember it. And they remember Maggie's mandolin, and they remember climbing over a highway median wall. Nothing was coming until a car was coming and left the boy in pieces. So the grandfather/reporter tells Goblin's story the best he can or there's no honor in it for the boy or the old man. Was Goblin living free or trapped by life? Brave or fearful, strong or weak? He was all of that, all those contradictory things that made his life a dazzling, dangerous, dismaying dance.

Then, in the summer of 2012, he had a chance to do the dance a different way.

After leaving Jacob in Myrtle Beach, Jared and Lyndzy spent two weeks at Jeff's home in Locust Grove, Virginia. They camped out on the front porch and slept in a backyard shed. They stayed that long because Jared's condition had deteriorated so badly that he woke up each morning coughing blood—until Jeff and his wife, Lisa, a registered nurse, persuaded him to go to her hospital for treatment. There he endured a week of detoxification that set off waves of DTs.

His winter at his mother's home, recovering from the Arizona accident, had given him a chance to change his life. Now he had a second chance. But even in his stepmother's hospital, he wanted what he'd wanted that long winter in Myrtle Beach. He wanted only to get back on the road. One evening he pulled himself to the edge of the bed and began unhooking IV tubes and monitor lines. "I gotta get out of here," he said. "I gotta go to the train station." No sooner did his feet touch the floor than a nurse, Charles Harrison, once a gunner's mate in the US Navy, said, "Dude, you ain't goin' anywhere until I say so."

Jared had ignored repeated warnings. Not this time. This time a week of relentless pain beat him down. With Lisa and Lyndzy encouraging him, he said he'd try to get sober. Jeff and Lisa did the preliminary work to have him admitted to Boxwood Recovery Center in Culpeper, Virginia. Then came the drive to Boxwood, thirty-six miles from Lisa's hospital.

She drove, Jared sat beside her, silent.

They drove ten miles, fifteen miles, twenty.

Abruptly ending the silence, Jared said, "Where's Lyndzy?"

Lisa didn't want to answer.

"I said, where *is* she? She wanted me to do this, where is *she*?"

Lyndzy had left Jeff's place the night before. She told Jeff she could no longer handle the bloody mornings. She said she couldn't wait for Jared to do the rehab. She had to leave. She would go to Fredericksburg and meet a friend.

Lisa said, "She went to find Patches."

"Patches? What the *fuck*! How'd he get in this? Turn around. Lisa, turn around."

"We're practically there," she said.

"Or I'm getting out."

Jared had said he would go, he knew he should go, and of such plans and promises and hopes are an addict's days and weeks and months filled. The addict says it all to make everyone feel better, to give everyone hope, to give himself hope, and yet, when it comes time, the addict's brain says no in fear of the pain coming with the DTs of detox. Before Lisa, loving him, could get him to Boxwood, Jared found a reason to say no, hearing about Patches, and he said no, he would not go.

"He'd been getting all agitated," Jeff said. "He wasn't his normal happy-go-lucky self because Lyndzy was leaving to go off with Patches and he just couldn't take it. He was jealous of that guy and didn't want her to leave. If she'd stayed, who knows? We were an inch away from getting him to Boxwood. But once she left, he couldn't do it. I should have just tied him down and made him go."

The sad truth is, convincing Jared was impossible. He no longer made his own decisions. The addiction decided for him. He was, literally, not in his right mind. That's not the theory of a grandfather loving a grandson. It's the finding of neuroscientists, psychologists, and drug abuse researchers who believe that addiction damages the parts of the brain responsible for judgment. They say the last person to know his brain is broken is the person whose brain is broken.

David Sheff, a journalist, is a rock star among addiction experts. *Time* magazine placed him among the world's one hundred most influential people in 2013. In his book *Clean: Overcoming Addiction and Ending America's Greatest Tragedy*, Sheff explains alcohol's effect on the brain:

> When drugs are withheld, the brain goes into a kind of shock. The system is starved for dopamine and other neurotransmitters. It's not quite as serious as oxygen deprivation, but it can feel like that—as if death is imminent. In distress, the entire body system now has one purpose: to return to equilibrium by finding more drugs to stimulate dopamine flow. Addicts can feel as if they're fighting for their lives, and they may be . . . cells are dying and neurons misfiring, which can cause tremors, nausea, anxiety, hallucinations, fever, and disorientation. But that's not all. The heart rate can rise dangerously, and the addict has a high risk of seizures, which are sometimes fatal. . . . Detoxing from alcohol is particularly dangerous.

Alcohol is the deadliest drug. It kills insidiously. The body converts alcohol into a poison, acetaldehyde, that passes through the liver into the bloodstream, where it damages every organ it touches. In thirty seconds, the poison reaches the brain. It's like cutting a lamp's cord. Electricity doesn't get through anymore. It's dark. Regions of the brain can't talk to each other. Confusion ensues. All this is going on quietly.

The big noise is the party. Even as the poison eats away at the white matter, it also sets loose a flood of dopamine, a feel-good chemical. Anything a person likes—food, sex, gambling, vodka—can start dopamine flowing. The more poison in an alcoholic's brain, the more he likes it. Enough of it, he feels good, confident, powerful, sexy. More than enough, he is a bulletproof freakin' god. Past that, he is blackout drunk on the way to coma.

The liver, awash in alcohol, produces acetaldehyde quickly and acetate slowly. Acetate is a feel-bad acid that sends most of us looking for a place to throw up. We stop drinking when the alcoholic is just getting warmed up.

The alcoholic's big trouble comes when the brain adapts to the poison. Then, to get that bulletproof feeling, he needs more alcohol than before. The longer this escalation goes on, the greater the need. The brain is so numbed that not only is there no buzz when he's drinking, but the alcoholic no longer feels normal when he's not drinking. Now the drinking is more than a matter of feeling good. Now it feels like life and death. His brain is now physically dependent on alcohol. Without alcohol, it will shut down. The alcoholic will suffer the DTs, withdrawal, blackouts, seizures.

Now you are an addict. Now you're no longer in charge of your drinking. Your brain gives you orders that you have no power to turn down, like, "Get off your ass and get us another half-gallon or we're going to die here." You must get alcohol across your tongue, down your throat, into your gut, through your liver, and into your brain. Or else it will never shut the fuck up.

So you and your brain go to the liquor store.

Every year in the United States, there are eighty-eight thousand deaths for which the primary cause is alcohol. The Centers for Disease Control and Prevention reports that alcohol-related deaths result in two and a half million years of life lost, an average of thirty years per person. Every year, eighty-eight thousand obituaries. Every year, millions of survivors diminished by the loss of loved ones.

Yes, Jared chose to drink. He did not, however, choose to be addicted. For all that science has learned about the brain and its workings, it remains a mystery all but divine in its complexities. Science tells us that some brains resist addiction while others are addicted from the start. Because there is a genetic link to alcoholism, Jared and Jacob were at risk from birth. Alcohol abuse was present in their immediate family history, from both their father and mother.

Jeff told me, "I guess I'm what they call now a 'functional alcoholic.' I've never drank at or during work, but when I do drink, I drink too much. Lynn drank too, but not as much as I did." He also said, "The boys would see me drinking. So I blame myself for a percentage of Jared's drinking. He just wouldn't quit. Jacob could handle it better." Jeff's idea of Jacob "handling it better" was nearly as frightening as Jared not handling it at all. "Jacob would get sick and quit."

Lynn's father, an alcoholic, died at sixty. She said, "I didn't drink nearly as often as Jeff, but when I did, I would almost always overdo it. I blame myself for Jared too, but not so much for drinking. If I hadn't moved to South Carolina, Jared would never have been on the street. He'd have never been the drinker he was. I told him, 'Smoke pot. Smoke all the pot you want. Get happy. Don't be stupid, don't destroy your liver.'"

It's too much to say I grew up in a tavern. But from around age six to fifteen, I stayed with my grandmother in Lincoln, Illinois, so I could play Little League baseball, and that meant I spent summer nights in Forehand's West Side Tavern. It stood on Sangamon Street along the Illinois Central Railroad tracks that passed by our house in Atlanta, ten miles north. Grandma Lena and her husband, Tommy Forehand, ran the place. My father built the tavern's bar. For customers with strong stomachs and bizarre tastes, there was a glass jar of pickled pigs' feet at the bar's far end. Men stood at the brass bar rail (four spittoons, cigarette butts floating in tobacco juice) and drank Pabst Blue Ribbon, Falstaff, Stag, and Schlitz. On New Year's Eve 1949, I was eight years old and danced with a woman named Flo, who pressed my head against her pink angora sweater and between her considerable breasts. A grand place that tavern.

I never drank—until I was eighteen and traveling with my college baseball team in New Orleans. As Booze Cop might put it, there's no need to be twenty-one on Bourbon Street, so a teenager goes straight to Pat O'Brien's. The saloon's famous drink is the Hurricane—four ounces of fruity rum and four ounces of O'Brien's special Hurricane mix over crushed ice in a twenty-six-ounce hurricane glass, garnished with an orange slice and a cherry. It's pretty, it's smooth, it tastes great, and no one can drink just one. I spent the night bent over the edge of my bed. I dizzy-walked through the next day's game, striking out three straight times against pitches that danced in blurred curlicues.

Beer made my sportswriter's world go round. It was a major sponsor of every big-time event, the foundation of stadiums across America. Two of *Sports Illustrated*'s stars, Frank Deford and Rick Reilly, appeared in beer commercials that added a "Great taste! Less filling!" element to sports journalism's Oscar Madison stereotype.

In Louisville, I worked with Clarence "Slick" Royalty. Though Slick couldn't write a note to the milkman, he was famous in our office, mostly because he rescued the great Grantland Rice on deadline at a Kentucky Derby. According to Slick, Granny had sipped two or three mint juleps too many. Slick became Granny's ghost, typing under the famous byline and shipping the result to New York. No one believed Slick's story. But everyone believed something like that had happened a thousand times. The *San Francisco Examiner*'s Wells Twombly began typing only after pouring two fingers of Scotch in a tumbler by his machine. The New

York sportswriter Jack Lang arranged a cross-country airplane charter for sportswriters at the World Series that became known as "Captain Jack's Flying Drunk Tank." Pete Axthelm of *Newsweek* was told that he'd die if he kept drinking. "Then I'm going to die," he said, "because I'm not stopping." He died at forty-seven.

Red Smith favored "razor blade soup," sometimes known as martinis. While in college, Jane Leavy, later my buddy at the *Washington Post*, did a profile on Red. Believing it a kind of duty—"The ethos was, sportswriters drank and never missed a deadline"—she delivered vodka to Red as he worked, with one instruction from the great man: "Hold the fruit." No lemon, no lime. She matched Red one-for-one, even at the airport, where they boarded a plane for New York. On arrival, Red couldn't find his car or even the parking lot. "Where's Lot 1?" he asked an airport worker. "No Lot 1," the man said, "only A, B, C." The problem was solved when Leavy realized they had landed in Newark. "We had flown to the wrong damn city," she said.

Leavy and I were among the American press corps en route to Sarajevo for the 1984 Winter Olympics. At a reception in Zagreb, our hosts supplied a vicious eastern European poison called slivovitz. It's a plum brandy that has been compared to lighter fluid, paint thinner, and jet fuel. One sip set my esophagus on fire. We boarded a train for a night ride through the mountains of Yugoslavia. Attempting to extinguish the fire in my throat, I drank beer for the next seven hours. I learned both the Serbo-Croatian word for beer and the name of the comely train attendant eager to serve us. Every half-hour or so, I heard myself cry out, "Piva, Behrka!"

One more story: After a day at the 1972 Olympics in Munich, my wife and I had a pitcher of beer at dinner. We then returned to a house we shared with other Americans. Deep into Southern Comfort, the men poured us each a half-glass of that sweet poison.

Damn, it went down easy and with results a wiser man would have anticipated. All night, despite my best efforts, my bed spun on a horizontal plane. I moved to a safer place, the floor. It too spun. My wife threw up multiple times. I never did. The poison stayed in my system through the next day at the Olympics. In an upset, I lived.

Never again, Hurricanes. Never again, slivovitz. Never again, "Piva, Behrka." Never again, Southern Comfort.

Jared seemed to have been quickly addicted to alcohol, perhaps as early as the day in Key West at age thirteen when he shared a pitcher of beer with Jacob. It started that way for Jay Davidson, an alcoholic in recovery who is now the chairman at The Healing Place, an alcohol abuse facility in Louisville, Kentucky.

"I was thirteen years old when I had my first taste of beer," Davidson said. "I liked it and I drank three more right then. My brain went, 'Wow, this is really good!'" He said that most men who ended up at The Healing Place "experienced, in adolescence, some kind of physical, emotional, psychological, spiritual pain. They had low self-esteem, shame, humiliation, despair. They've lived with those feelings most of their lives. So they drank. Alcoholics drink for one reason—to change the way we feel. Drinking gave me esteem and power. I was able to relate to the opposite sex. Once I started drinking, I wouldn't stop until I passed out. That's the point at which you have crossed over from abuse of the chemical to dependence on it."

Early intervention is a powerful tool against alcoholism, Davidson said—intervention at thirteen if necessary. "Family, friends, and everyone who loves the alcoholic has to intervene as soon as the signs are there. The intervention has to identify the one thing the alcoholic does not want to lose. There's something he doesn't want to lose. It could be a spouse, a job, a best friend. You must identify the fear of the loss of that one thing. And the intervention group has to be solid. If one person in the group says, 'Oh well, it was just one time, he'll get better,' guess who the alcoholic will listen to."

Once a person becomes dependent on alcohol, Davidson said, the only way out is through detoxification, rehabilitation, and abstinence, each of them a harrowing step toward sobriety. Even the first step, detox, is frightening. Many addicts prefer the high risk of continuing to use the substance to the certainty of delirium tremens and the possibility, even probability, of relapse after rehab and a need to go through it all again.

Jared had already spent a week of horror in his stepmother's hospital. Boxwood promised more. He said no.

ooooo

Refusing Boxwood, Jared went on the road again, first to Syracuse, New York, where in the summer of 2012 he met a street preacher named John Tumino.

Once a restaurant owner, Tumino had left the business world to create a charitable organization called In My Father's Kitchen. His work taught him that people walk by the homeless without seeing them—as if they're invisible. The author Peter Matthiessen, after his own street service, said, "I heard a homeless woman say, 'You know what we are to you people? We are like a piece of Kleenex that somebody's blown their nose into and thrown on the rainy sidewalk. Who wants to pick that up?'"

Tumino's mantra on street people became "You are not invisible!" It was his assurance to them and all those wandering on the fringes of society that they were seen by the only eyes that mattered, God's.

He met Jared and a Lakota Sioux named Ash Dogskin flying sign under a bridge. "They were nice guys, free spirits, lovers of life, sociable. There was a softness to them, they didn't have a mean streak."

Twice a week for two months, Tumino stopped to see them. "We fed and clothed them too, as well as providing things they needed to survive outdoors, sleeping bags, wet wipes, toiletries. But I made a point of not preaching against that dangerous life. My purpose was to share the gospel of Jesus Christ with your grandson. I only wanted him to hear about the love of Christ. He heard me, yes. Did he accept it? I believe he did. I believe in the power of Jesus Christ."

By 2018, twenty-one of the homeless people Tumino took care of had died, including a woman beaten to death a quarter-mile from Jared's panhandling spot.

ooooo

From Syracuse, Jared worked his way west to Ann Arbor, Michigan, where he again wound up in a hospital. There, not for the first time, but in the most dramatic way, a doctor told him that drinking would kill him.

Jared had rolled off a park bench during a seizure. The University of Michigan Health System report identified him as a twenty-three-year-old man with a history of alcohol withdrawal seizures.

> The patient is currently traveling (hopping on and off carrier trains) to Pittsburgh with two friends. States the three of them consume between ½ gallon of vodka or a box of wine daily. . . . Initial labs additionally demonstrated pancreatitis, transaminitis, and acute kidney injury . . . (with symptoms of) tremulousness, anxiety, hallucinations, diaphoresis, tachycardia, . . . and hypertension.

A CT scan of his brain showed "advanced volume loss for the patient's stated age" and "encephalomalacia involving the left frontal lobe." The volume loss was likely attributable to alcohol abuse. Encephalomalacia, a softening of brain tissue, usually occurs after an injury. The citing of brain injury reinforced the New Orleans hospital's report of a cavitary defect in the left frontal lobe—the brain's home of reason, judgment, and emotion. Maybe that defect allowed Jared to leave the hospital "against medical advice" (AMA).

> Throughout his hospital course, the patient threatened to leave AMA several times, eventually leaving AMA on 8/30 after a thorough discussion of the risks . . . (including but not limited to death, seizure, brain damage, sepsis, and organ dysfunction). The patient signed AMA paperwork.

For Yossi Holoshitz, the attending physician, Jared's case was personal. He told me, "I made a mental note, he was the same age as my daughter." Holoshitz remembered the unique elements of Jared's admission. The youth. The multiple seizures. The travelers, Ash Dogskin and Jersey Guy, staying at Jared's bedside. "Here were these young people," Holoshitz said, "undergoing this kind of rough life."

Holoshitz wanted Jared to stay in the hospital. "I told him, 'You're putting your life in danger. You're young, you have many years ahead of you if you take care of yourself.'"

Jared was not cooperative.

"He didn't talk at any length," the doctor said.

Holoshitz was so taken by Jared's circumstances that he did an extraordinary thing. For the first time in his memory, he made a telephone call to a patient's mother. Then Lynn called me. Her

voice was flat. Of all our conversations—beginning with her sobbing report of Jared's facial tattoo—this one was memorable for its
melancholy.

She said, "Dr. Holoshitz told me that if Jared didn't quit drinking, he'd die."

In clinical language, the New Orleans hospital had warned
Jared of the risk of drinking. Now, seventeen months later, a doctor
had delivered the cold truth himself. Holoshitz's words suggested
inevitability.

What do we do, then? Jared had so consistently resisted all our
pleadings that we believed he would change his life only, in the
terrible phrase, "when he hit bottom." If being told you'd kill yourself by drinking was not hitting bottom, what was? He had been
run over by a car. That changed nothing. He had been beaten until
his brain bled. That changed nothing. He had been in a Virginia
hospital for a week of detox. That changed nothing. And if nothing
changed, the chilling, frightening truth was that Dr. Holoshitz's
warning would no longer be a warning—it would be fact.

It is easy to say we should have found Jared and carried him
to a detox and rehab center. His father couldn't get it done even
when he was within "an inch" of getting it done. Maybe we should
have hunted him down, bound him, gagged him, kidnapped him
from his road dogs, and delivered him to an alcohol abuse facility.
Have him legally committed against his will, effectively imprison
him? The hard, cold truth—as I would learn years later from David Sheff and Jay Davidson—is that if an addict doesn't give himself up to the long-term agony of gaining sobriety, outside forces
are helpless.

All we did, then, was the same old lame-ass begging him to
quit drinking. He said he was cutting down. We knew better. We
knew he made promises that he couldn't keep. We knew he knew

he was lying. So we just shut up. Short of legal commitment—unthinkable, nearly impossible to accomplish—we could do nothing for a young man we loved.

ooooo

On the road, turning south to South Holston Lake in northeastern Tennessee, Jared went to an annual event called a Rainbow Gathering.

One of a dozen Gatherings across the United States, it drew twenty thousand hippies and hoboes, the homeless and the wandering. There, four months after putting together Sarafina Scarlet's wedding, Jared again saw Maggie, the girl with the mandolin.

By then, Maggie had been on the road five years. Her fine little face matched Jared's. Her phone ringtone was a night train's lonesome whistle. Her Facebook page let readers know that she "Started Work as Professional Bum 2008." She had hitchhiked from home in North Carolina to California. She worked as an inventory clerk for a moving company until she earned enough money to fly back to Charleston, South Carolina. From there, she hopped her first train, Charleston to Waycross, Georgia. She seldom sat still long.

Maggie's movements, per FB:

Knoxville, Fucking Indiana, Pittsburgh hawking for hamburgers, In Philly, Wisconsinnnn, Minnesota, Los Angeles babyyyy, New Mexico! TEXAS!!! San AntonioNO, AUSTIN!! Louisiana-bound goodbye dallas, North Dakota, Augusta Georgia, In Maryland . . .

A note in there:

sharing a forty is like watching a stripper take off her shoes, a pointless, teasing waste of money.

Another:

What did you expect, a sunday morning saint? An optimistic troubadour
from this pessimistic sleaze? Sure I change for the worse and baby I'm
never coming back

At the Rainbow Gathering, she noticed Jared right away, the
wedding fresh in her memory. Besides, how could she miss him?
"He was being goofy, talking silly, just dancing around, hoppity-
hoppy, being all silly with hand gestures and noises, just happy. He
was the happiest guy I'd ever seen."

ELEVEN

They were a glamour couple in their world of grit and grime: Maggie with the black dreads, brown eyes, and the faintest of tattoo lines across her cheekbones; Goblin the small, blond, blue-eyed flirt with the badass face tattoo. They might have been figurines atop a hoboes' wedding cake, bride and groom, living happily ever after in blackened, patched, greasy Carhartt bibs. For Maggie, it was what she thought love should be. "He made me laugh," she said, "and he made me feel safe."

When Jared called home, his mother heard a difference in his voice. "He was so excited, more so than I'd ever known him to be," Lynn said. "So in love with Maggie." It was Lynn's theory that Jared would come back to the real world when he found the right girl. With the right one, his mother thought, Jared could settle down, get off the road, have a life.

Maggie said, "We were like two best friends who loved each other and traveled the country together. We lived under bridges and in skywalks and pastures and hotels and friends' houses and on trains. We ate gas station food on food stamps and out of dumpsters where they'd thrown good food away. One time we went to TGIF for all-you-could-eat and all we could eat was $5 worth. Just not used to eating."

Most travelin' kids move in pairs for company and safety. As Maggie did with her Dixie, they also often take along a dog for the extra security of a light sleeper who promises to wake up barking at an intruder in the night. Because they live moment-to-moment, dependent on kindnesses, they share the primal necessities of life on the road: shelter, sleep, food, drink, sex.

Maggie and Jared also shared vodka. "Like water for us," she said. Taaka. McCormick. Skol. Popov. Nikolai. "The smart kids do vodka, it's cheaper than whiskey. Bottom-shelf, $11.49 before taxes, $12.50 out the door. One and a half gallons a day, if it was just Jared and me. It'd be gone in ten hours, that's if we're sippin' it slow. We wouldn't get shit-faced, just a steady flow of alcohol in our systems to avoid the DTs. Whatever was cheapest was Jared's favorite. He'd drink it straight up, sometimes he'd chase it with orange or blue Powerade. Or he'd say, 'I chase with my spit on the Mississip'."

"There's plenty of people who don't drink out here. Either they don't drink, or know what they're capable of, or are smarter, or are overcoming alcoholism. Jared loved drinking with his friends. He'd be more social, more talkative. He'd function better with a buzz on."

Early in October of 2012, they used Facebook to let their road dogs know the news:

Jared Kindred and Mags N Dixie are in a Relationship

She loved silly things about him. The way he told her, "I've got your back like a butt crack." His goofy rhymes: "Nation station explanation!" "Nig nog, niggity noggity niggity." "Jont-ja-jont." "Maxin' and relaxin'." "Skibbity bee bop um bee." She pronounced a road dog's version of wedding vows: "Hospital visits, whether yours or mine, we were there for each other in sickness or in health and in good or bad."

She added, "You want to hear his favorite joke? A duck walks into a bar and asks, 'Got any grapes?' The bartender says no. The next day, the duck asks again, 'Got any grapes?' The bartender says, 'No grapes, we've never had grapes, we never will have grapes, and if you ask for grapes again, I'll nail your stupid duck bill to the bar.' The duck thinks about that and asks, 'Got any nails?' The bartender says no, he's got no nails. 'Good,' the duck says. 'Got any grapes?'"

Maggie said, "If he'd wanted to get married, get settled, get jobs, I'd have said, 'Where do I sign up?' If he'd said, 'I'll quit this, I just want to have a place,' that would've been it. I'd have married him in a fuckin' heartbeat."

Maggie was the right one.

With her, maybe Jared could find his way.

ooooo

Jared had slogged through Hurricane Irene the year before. Now, in late October 2012, he and Maggie arrived in Philadelphia as Hurricane Sandy neared landfall on the New Jersey coast. One night they took shelter in a honeycombed concrete wall. Jared entertained Maggie with stories about World War II. She said, "Four hours, nonstop, off the damn History Channel! Nazis! Panzer tanks! Eisenhower, D-Day. I thought that war would never end."

He had his own war going on. He called later with that story. "We stopped at a Wawa gas station. I wanted a Gatorade, thought that might help. My chest hurt really, really, really bad. I didn't know what it was, what was wrong, it just hurt really, really, really bad. For some magical reason, an ambulance was at the Wawa too. I knocked on the window and asked them to take me to a hospital."

A heart attack? His family had a history of heart troubles. My father's father died of heart disease. I have coronary artery disease. My son has atrial fibrillation. Jared had been diagnosed with tachy-cardia, a condition that causes the heart to race, sometimes at two hundred beats a minute, less a rhythmic beating than a high-rev thrum. Was it a heart attack, or was Jared about to have a seizure? Maggie had seen seizures happen: "He'd get that blank stare. He knew it was coming. Just staring. I yelled, 'Goblin!' He wouldn't even blink. Like he didn't hear nothing. 'Goblin, Goblin, look at me!' Nothing. And he'd start shaking, these really hard full-body twitches. And he'd be making really weird noises. And then he'd fall over. Out of it. That's when we called 911."

As he did with increasing regularity, Jared called me. He said doctors at Nazareth Hospital "gave me a little white pill, a muscle-relaxer or something, I don't know what the hell they gave me. They said I should stay for three or four days, to detox and get into rehab."

I asked, "Are you still in the hospital?"

"Fuck no. I already checked myself out."

He said it hard and fast, as if it were the only possible answer, as if that magical ambulance had delivered him into enemy terri-tory, as if he had to get out of there as fast as damn possible.

I said, "Jared, what are you thinking? You gotta get back in that hospital. You can't be on the street now."

"Grandpa, I ain't doin' no detox," he said.

I shut up about the hospital. There is no talking to an addict, even your grandson, once he's made up his mind to keep being an addict. I said, "Just call me when you get somewhere safe."

Again he had checked out AMA. As he had left Dr. Holoshitz in Ann Arbor, now he left Nazareth. Again, a hospital had given him what he needed, immediate relief from withdrawal. This time he rejected detoxification and rehabilitation so adamantly that he walked out without his clothes, which hospital staff had taken because they were covered with lice. He left in a hospital-issue wraparound gown and socks. Against all reason, and with a hurricane coming, he left a hospital AMA wearing a cotton wraparound gown and socks.

Maggie was with him. To get help, she called the only person she knew in Philadelphia, a sixty-two-year-old Chinese American who had befriended the couple earlier that week. John Wong said he had been "intrigued by the tattoos on Jared's face." He was also curious about lives that put such young people on the street. "I learned they were kids who liked to ride trains, they were 'traveling kids.' They were good kids."

Wong supplied Jared with clothes and then came up with a pair of shoes that, even two sizes too large, were an improvement over socks. With Maggie at his side, Jared spent the night sleeping behind a Social Security building.

And then he was gone. He had awakened and wandered off, leaving Maggie behind. From 6:00 a.m. until nearly 11:00 p.m. on the day Hurricane Sandy arrived in Philadelphia, Maggie couldn't find him. In that time, the storm delivered 1.82 inches of rain. Winds reached sixty-two miles per hour. The low temperature was fifty-one degrees.

Those mystified by his disappearance included Jared himself. The first word of his whereabouts came in a phone call to his mother, but he couldn't tell her much. Lynn sounded at once frightened and relieved when she made yet one more late-night phone call to me with one more piece of harrowing news: "Jared said he was at a CVS pharmacy in West Philly somewhere. He had no idea how he'd gotten there or how long he'd been walking. It had to have been one hellacious walk from where he'd been, at the Social Security building, clear across town."

He had walked in hurricane-driven rain and in wind chills below freezing. He was likely disoriented by bottom-shelf vodka mixed with drugs the hospital had administered. He was so lost that he told his mother, "I'm looking for Maggie."

So Lynn called Maggie, who in turn called Wong, who picked her up and drove with her around Philadelphia in search of that CVS store and Jared.

"He just took off from where they'd been," Wong said. "We heard he headed to West Philadelphia through a tough, black neighborhood where it wasn't safe to be going. To get over to that CVS, he had to take an elevated train or just walk for hours. We got over there and walked up and down the street for a couple hours. Then he finally showed his face."

"I don't remember leaving Maggie," Jared told me that night on the phone. "I was really confused."

"You remember anything at all?"

"I remember talking to people who weren't there."

"Jared."

"I know, Grandpa."

"You okay now?"

"I'm feeling better," he said. "I'm not brain-dead retarded anyhow."

My grandson. Talking to hallucinations. Happy to be un-brain-dead. I hear him say so. I want to howl and wail. I want to scream and pray. I want to change what's happening. I do none of it. I do nothing because by now I know nothing changes anything. We have fallen into a darkness so dark it admits no light, ever.

I go for a laugh.

"From now on, boy, do me two favors."

"Yeah?"

"Cut out the vodka."

"I know."

"And stay out of hurricanes."

ooooo

My notes record another conversation two months later, on December 4, 2012. Jared and Maggie had gone from Philadelphia to her mother, Kayla's, house in Mount Airy, a little town in the Appalachian foothills of North Carolina.

"I'm feeling all right now, not terrible," he said.

A grandpa sermon number infinity: "You gotta quit drinking."

"Me and Maggie are cutting down."

"Way down, like to nothing, okay?"

"We're not having any more passing out. No more seizures."

"Good, keep it up."

"Yeah, seizures are no fun."

Alcoholics lie. They lie to friends, family, and themselves. They lie to preserve the opportunity to drink again. I knew the alcoholic's need to lie. I knew it when I made those notes on that December day in 2012. But Jared was my grandson. Sometimes we believe what we want to believe rather than what is believable, and I wanted to believe Jared could be an exception, that he could tell me the truth, and maybe he did tell me the truth. But I learned he didn't tell me the whole truth.

The whole truth would have included an accounting of the road trip from hell.

MAGGIE'S STORY

It was about the middle of November in 2012. I had this friend with cerebral palsy who needed someone to drive her from Charlotte to Houston. Could we do that? She'd pay me and Jared $100. We would deliver her to her boyfriend's house and then drive her car back to North Carolina.

So we drove her to Houston. The second day there, the trouble started. Jared gets sick and the bitch gets into a fight with her boyfriend and wants us to take her back to Charlotte right now.

She had given us only $50 on the way, with the other $50 to come later. But we'd spent the $50 getting to Houston. So now we don't have any money and Jared's too sick to go fly sign himself. I have to go out and make money to eat before we take off back to North Carolina. It's a thousand fuckin' miles.

Within five hours of driving east, Jared's starting to puke some blood and we're still in Texas and it's night and it's two o'clock in the morning before we get a hotel. The puking's not bad yet, I thought, until I saw some dark stains on the floor. Jared said it was spit, and I said, "Spit doesn't leave dark stains. That's blood. If it gets worse, we gotta get to a hospital," and he said, "No, no, I'll be okay."

It got worse as we drove through the next day, and it kept getting worse, and I'm driving with the bitch in the front seat complaining that Jared's messing up her car, and Jared's in the back seat sounding like he's dying, puking blood everywhere, all over himself.

I'm driving balls-to-the-wall with one hand on the steering wheel's suicide knob and reaching back to hold Jared's head up and feeling for a pulse and now she's complaining that I'm driving crazy.

I scream at her, "What do you want? What do you want? You keep it up, I'm gonna dump you out right here and you can fuckin' walk to Charlotte."

She says, "Calm down," and I say, "Fuck you! I am not gonna calm down! Leave me alone, let me drive." Then she makes me stop somewhere to buy her a cheeseburger.

Now I'm calling Mom from Louisiana, "What should I do?" and she's calling me every hour to keep me awake and we're near Spartanburg, South Carolina, and I tell her to meet us at the bitch's house in Charlotte. Now I've been driving for eighteen hours or something, and we get to the house in Charlotte and what's the bitch's parents do when they see Jared and the blood? They won't let us come in the house. Jared's going, "I'm making so much noise, I'm sorry," and I tell him, "Puke louder!"

It's four o'clock in the morning, and it's thirty degrees, and we have to wait there in the dark. Mom wants to take us to ER in Charlotte, but I figure we'll have to wait all night. She picks us up and we head for the Mount Airy hospital, ninety miles away.

As we leave, I'm screaming at the bitch, "Give me our $50!"

Kayla's Story

The ride from Charlotte to Mount Airy was one of the worst nights of my life. All the way, I was so impressed with Maggie's devotion to taking care of Jared. He was covered with blood, he'd been vomiting, there was this awful smell. Maggie was catching the blood in cups and she was pulling vomit from his mouth. He'd say, "I'm so sorry, I'm so sorry," and we'd try to comfort him the best we could.

I was driving as fast as I could without crashing. I thought he might die in the car. There was Maggie on her knees in the front seat reaching back to hold his head up. She'd be saying, "Another hour, baby, hang in there."

She was totally focused on him even after two and a half days of driving. She wasn't going to let him die. She loved him, man, she loved *him to do all that, and I saw a different Maggie than I'd ever seen. She wasn't just some cold bitch who wouldn't talk to me. We were in this together.*

And once we got to the hospital, she helped him walk in there, and she was there every day, all day, for the next however many days until he was well enough to come to the house.

TWELVE

Maggie and Jared had planned to stay at her mother's house only briefly and then be on their way to warmer weather. Instead, when Jared left the hospital, they came to a stop. They spent the winter in Mount Airy. For the first time in years, because Kayla wouldn't allow booze in the house, they weren't drunk 24/7, or even much at all. The months in North Carolina were so pleasant that the wanderers allowed themselves to imagine a life off the road.

We hear sometimes what we want to hear. When I heard Jared, in a phone call from Mount Airy, say, "We'll be here a while," I heard a whisper of hope in that simple, beautiful sentence. I hoped he was tired of the running and the drinking and the pain. I hoped he had heard the concern in Dr. Holoshitz's warning and the love in John Tumino's preaching.

We see sometimes what we want to see. I saw hope in the form of a kitten. Jared told me that one day, shortly after leaving the hospital, he was sitting on Kayla's front porch. A kitten, small and golden, solitary and trembling, climbed onto his lap. The boy had grown up with cats because his mother had a houseful, as many as six at a time. Lynn said, "I spoiled 'em so rotten that Jared always said, 'When I come back, Mom, I want to come back as one of your cats.'" Jared gave this little golden cat a name, Spud, and he took her into the house to stay. I hoped Spud reminded him of home and his mother, and I hoped Spud would be a reason that Jared might stay in Mount Airy longer than a while.

He liked it in Kayla's house. "Pretty cool here," he said. "Maggie's mom has two dogs, named Fiona and Ruby. You'd like them. They look like Hercules and Jackson." Hercules was his father's dog, black and burly. Jackson was our dog, a red-coated stray that came out of the woods to our house and stayed. We believe what we want to believe. I believed, in that moment when he spoke of two scruffy dogs in Virginia, that he wanted to be with us, to be home.

Jared also reported the day's big news: Maggie had shined up her mandolin.

"It was dirty?" I said.

"She's been carrying it places." A laugh here. "She loves that mandolin. She likes that green color. It's really green. It's a super-green mandolin. She really really likes green."

For once, Maggie was happy to be in Mount Airy. She had spoken to her mother only by phone, and only two or three times, since her release five years earlier from the local juvenile detention center. She'd already led a peripatetic adolescence. She was ten years old when her father left home for good. She declared herself happy with his departure because he was "a southern redneck dude. All he did was get drunk and watch NASCAR and wrestling on TV." Yet, after her parents divorced, Maggie lived on Long Island with the father, then a car salesman. The daughter of a southern redneck dude didn't fit in well at a Queens high school with "the Jewish American Princesses and their limousines." But Maggie loved the city. "New York! All the punks in the world! I partied my ass off." After returning to Mount Airy for her senior year ("which did not come out well"), she blew off one school, transferred to two others, and wound up in that detention center. Her offense? "Getting in trouble."

In those years, Mount Airy had nothing for her. The small town in the foothills of the Appalachians is remarkable only as the hometown of actor Andy Griffith. It sells itself as the model for Mayberry, the setting of Griffith's iconic television show. Maggie never visited the Andy Griffith Museum (with a statue of Andy and Opie going fishing). She never ate at Barney's Cafe or watched a haircut at Floyd's Barber Shop. What she did mostly was leave Mount Airy for anywhere else.

This time was different. She was excited about being there. For reasons she couldn't explain, "least of all to myself," she wanted her mother to meet this guy Goblin.

On January 3, 2013, Jared and Maggie walked up bare wooden stairs to their all-time champion of unlikely sleeping places—the unfinished attic above Kayla's bedroom.

Kayla had repurposed the space from storage to a quilting room. Now, for the wanderers who might spend the winter, she made it over into a bedroom. Maggie and Jared dropped a mattress on the floor, brought up a desk and a small chest of drawers, and draped an American flag on a wall. As near to a home as they had known in years, the little room in Mount Airy was an escape from their escapes.

Maggie had had other boyfriends. Kayla never liked them. But she wasn't afraid of this one. Jared was courteous and sweet, but she also saw him as slight and frail, vulnerable. He needed to be nursed back to health. She said, "We even went to the Earle together, just me and Jared." At the Earle, the old movie theater on Main Street, they saw *Lincoln*. "Afterwards," Kayla said, "he told me Civil War stories."

He did the dishes. No one asked him to do the dishes. He did them because he wanted to do them. "Not now," he said after dinner. "I'll do 'em in the morning," and every morning at seven thirty he did the dishes. If Kayla asked him to do something around the house, he did it. "If I asked him to dump the compost whenever he had a chance, he'd jump up from the table and do it right then."

Mornings, he would feed Spud, Dixie, Fiona, and Ruby. He would do the dishes and make himself a bowl of cereal. Then he would have another bowl of cereal, and another. "I'd eat a lot of cereal and a lot of milk," he told me one day, "because there was nothing else to do."

Kayla's mother had one rule for Jared and Maggie. No drinking in her house. She had been in that dark place with a husband, and she had been there with her daughter and Jared in a car, blood everywhere. No drinking, she said. Each day she looked for bottles under the attic mattress, and she checked the kitchen trash for bottles, and she never found a bottle.

"The couple weeks that Jared was in the hospital, detoxing," Maggie said later, "I'd drink only half of a half-gallon of vodka, trying to get myself off it for when he came home. He wanted to drink, and he would've if I did. But if I drank then, I'd be such a dick. I didn't drink so he wouldn't. I was able to do okay, so he was okay.

"It took him a while, though. He was pissed off at first and said, 'I want to keep drinking.' I said, 'You're really sick this time. I'll help you get through this, but I won't support, like, killing you.'

It was hard, I won't lie to you. He was really pissed. I let him holler at me, and I told him, 'You're not going to do anything to cause me to not be in your life.'"

No vodka. Then, one Friday night, Jared went to Kayla asking if they might, please, have a beer.

"No," she said.

"Just one," he said.

"I said no."

"Come *on*, it's *Friday night*!"

"No."

He left the house. Maggie told her mother not to worry, to let him cool off, he'd be back in a half-hour. And he was.

They settled on one forty-ounce beer a week. They bought it at the Red Barn, a convenience store operated by Mexican immigrants that was a stop on their daily walks with the dogs, Dixie dragging Jared around the neighborhood. They said they split the forty.

Sometimes the world they had left would insinuate itself into the attic hideaway. The road dogs' grapevine reached them in March 2013 with rumors of a murder in California. Some travelin' kids beat the shit out of a teenager and left him to die. One name Jared knew, Eddo, a kid he'd met in New Orleans. He didn't know the other names on the grapevine, Jewls and Aggro.

Maggie said, "Damn."

Jared said, "Dumb shits."

Every couple weeks, he called his Fairfax friend and urban-survival mentor, Michael Stephen.

Stephen said, "In the beginning at Mount Airy, he was bored and fidgety and didn't know what to do with himself. Later he would call, all happy about how he woke up at sunrise and made breakfast, did the dishes, and didn't know what to do next, so he made coffee and breakfast for everyone else, and then didn't know what to do next, so he cleaned up for them, cleaned the kitchen, went outside, did yard work, took a break, watched some TV, and when everyone had left, he started cleaning the house.

"I was really proud of him. I would say, 'See? Without the booze, it reveals what kind of person you are, Jared. Helpful, courteous, decent, a good person.' He was happy, proud of himself."

Stephen remembered a telephone conversation as Jared sat outside a Chinese restaurant.

"I could hear Maggie say something about the Chinese newspaper machine," Stephen said. "And Jared said, 'That's not Chinese, that's Korean.' Then, sort of to himself in shock, he said, 'How the fuck did I know that?' I told him, 'Jared, you knew that because you're really smart. Smarter than the average person. And a helluva lot smarter than you give yourself credit for. If you weren't smart as fuck, I wouldn't be your friend.'"

Jared was also working with a carpenter, Butch, a friend of Kayla's who had done work on her house.

"It was winter," Butch said, "but all he ever wore were those bib overalls, no shirt under them, and it never seemed to bother him. I paid him $10 an hour and picked him up at the house every morning. We had great conversations on the way to the job, mostly about his travels. He was a wandering man."

At Fries, Virginia, a half-hour north of Mount Airy, Butch and Jared built a porch on a house. "He worked with the chop saw—a saw on a miter box—and he could do anything I showed him. One day we were having a problem with the porch, and he suggested a way to do it different. And he was right. Bright kid and good worker."

"Butch is fun to work with," Jared told me in a call. "He's old and he wants to teach me stuff. That problem with the porch, I told him, 'Why don't we run the joists this way instead of that?' It worked out. We were happy that day."

Nights in Mount Airy, if you're twenty-four years old and trying to save money and trying not to drink after years of drinking every day, what do you do?

"Grandpa," Jared said, "I saw a used Xbox for sale. Only $200."

"I'll send you a check."

"I'll get me some overalls for the summer too," he said, "because all I have are these insulated ones for winter."

It was all good news. Jared in Mount Airy was the Jared we had known. Better yet, on February 28, 2013, he said, "I went to the doctor yesterday. My blood pressure is great, and my kidneys are doing perfect. He pretty much told me I'm really healthy."

Kayla hoped Jared had found reason to stop traveling. "His attitude had evolved. He had been someone who had no goal. Why that was, I don't know, but he felt he had all these strikes against him when, in fact, everyone admired him. He had been someone who didn't care from one day to the next. And while he was here, he became this guy who, 'If I get disability, Maggie, we could be together, I'd work with Butch, you get a job, we'd settle somewhere.'"

Maggie and Jared, in the attic room, talked in the night. It wasn't Kerouac longing for a different life and writing, "I want to marry a girl so I can rest my soul with her till we both get old. This can't go on all the time—all this franticness and jumping around. We've got to go someplace, find something." It was better than that. Maggie and Jared were looking for more than an end to the moment's franticness that would return him to a life he once knew. Maggie and Jared dared to imagine themselves becoming different people leading lives they had never known.

Maggie said, "We talked about 'Let's get our own place, settle down, get off the road, have friends over.'"

Jared's thinking had taken such a dramatic turn that I heard him for the first time talk of plans that extended beyond the next hop-out.

He said, "Maggie and me are trying to save up and get a truck or car. I think we'll be here a while, so I'm trying for disability now too. I saw an ad for a job that sounded interesting. I forget what they called it, but it was like being the super of a building. Fix stuff, live there for free. I just put in an application at a fast-food place too, and Maggie's talking about going to school for welding."

Welding?

Welding.

Maggie's talking about welding?

Welding never sounded so lovely.

In Myrtle Beach, Lynn heard the talk. Her sons were twenty-four years old. Neither had been close to marriage. But now Jared, in Mount Airy, talked about a future with the beautiful welder named Maggie. That was enough for Lynn, as it had been enough for me twenty-six years earlier when she stood at my desk in Georgia and asked if it was okay to marry my son. Lynn's response to the happy talk from Mount Airy was different from my response to her only in that she didn't get specific about gender or number or time of delivery. She just said, "I was thinking, 'Grandbabies!' And I'd spoil 'em rotten."

THIRTEEN

As content as Jared and Maggie were in North Carolina—like Lynn, I reveled in their joy—they had nothing on Mom in Illinois that same winter. One day she rolled her wheelchair along a hallway of her nursing home. At the end of the hall, she turned to look back to the other end. There she said an odd thing, as mothers sometimes do if they are lucky enough, and brave enough, to get really old. She looked down that long, smooth, shiny corridor and said, "I wish I had roller skates."

After escaping with her life from a hospital where a doctor had pronounced her condition as indicative of "the end of life," Mom had regained energy and enthusiasm. Her standard greeting for visitors at the nursing home became, "I'm still here, believe it or not." A physical therapist called her "my superstar" and reported that Mom, from her wheelchair, "was doing can-can kicks." A man who lived in a room next to hers formalized Mom's reputation as the nursing home's happiest camper. "She's our gigglebox," he said.

Here was Gigglebox, now ninety-five years old, wishing she could strap on a pair of skates and go swooshing down the hall the way she had once rattled down sidewalks. Her enthusiasm would have been remarkable at any age, in any place. It was extraordinary on this day because she lived with the knowledge that a lump in her left breast was most likely cancer.

Mom didn't see much reason to get excited. She had outlived two husbands, and she lived with really really old people, some of whom were at dinner one day and gone the next. She understood death was on its way, and if it was not all that welcome a visitor, it did no good to think the front door could be closed against it. I remembered that day in the Restmor dining room when she declared her agreement with fate: "When I'm old enough to die, I'll die."

We're all dying. It's part of the deal. The people who do it best live during the dying. Others, frightened by what they cannot escape, die during the living. Montaigne wrote that a "contempt of death" produces "a soft and easy tranquility, and gives us a pure and pleasant taste of living."

Mom's tranquility included her decision to be done with hospitals. The nursing home's visiting doctor had proposed a biopsy to determine if Mom did in fact have cancer. My sister, Sandra, who had been at Mom's side daily for a decade, immediately said no. No biopsy. No tests. Never another hospital. She said, "I promised Mom that." Then Sandra laughed. "Anyway, Mom was at the age where she kept forgetting she had cancer."

A woman born during World War I could be forgiven for forgetting a detail here and there. Besides, the nursing home activities staff kept her busy. Mondays: arts and crafts. Tuesdays: cooking club. Wednesdays: hairstyling. Thursdays: for the first time in her life, she had her nails done. Fridays: garden club. Saturdays: Catholic communion with her nursing home sidekick, Lena Vignieri.

Sundays: church services by assorted denominations. All this along with musical interludes, visits by local entertainers, physical therapy, movies with popcorn, bingo, and Scrabble. (Bless her, she loved wordplay.) Come September, in Morton, in the stinkweed hamlet that insisted it was the world's leading provider of pumpkins, Mom and Lena rolled along the Pumpkin Festival parade route in their wheelchairs, tossing candy to the spectators.

Forever a baseball fan, Mom wore her pink Cubs shirt to the annual Cubs-Cardinals Nerf-ball game in the nursing home's hospitality room. I was the umpire, and Mom thought she perceived a bias in favor of the Cardinals. "Your fault," I said, "for letting me stay up all those nights listening to Harry Caray."

I believe Mom simply ignored the cancer in her breast rather than give it the satisfaction of having disturbed her. She tolerated a morphine patch for the early stages of pain and later accepted more powerful medicine. Every day she knew where this was headed. But there was never a day when she wept, never a day when she asked anyone to feel sorry for her.

In her last years, I heard her express only one wish.

"Before I die," she said, "I want the Cubs to be in the World Series again."

Dying, she was living.

ooooo

She had learned that trick in 1963.

Dad showed her.

Marie Magdalena Maloney was twenty years old when she married John David Kindred, age twenty-five, a truck driver, carpenter, and cabinetmaker from Atlanta, Illinois. They had met in Lincoln when she worked as a short-order cook at her mother's restaurant, the Midway, a stop along Route 66. I was their first child, and Sandra came a year later. We lived in that Atlanta house by railroad tracks running parallel to 66. I loved that house and I love it still. It will always belong to Sandy and me. We will keep it because Dad told us that however old we might be, whatever our circumstances, we always had a place to live, always a home with him and Mom. Even now, an old man, I sit on the landing at the bottom of the steps leading up to the bedroom where, once upon a warm and safe time, at about ten every night, a freight train rumbled past our house. If only Jared had slept in such a place.

We owned all of a city block. Our house sat on one corner of it. Because I couldn't get enough baseball, Dad created our own ball diamond on the south side of the property. He chopped out stumps, carried away stones, and leveled the ground with chain-link fencing weighted down by cinder blocks and pulled behind his black 1950 Ford pickup with the *oogah-oogah* horn. During a period when I thought to be a pitcher, Dad contrived to build an aid to my control. He drove two wood lathings into the ground and stretched two strands of twine between them; one strand was tied at shoulder height and the other at the knees, with two more pieces of string set seventeen inches apart connecting the top and bottom strands. A strike, then, was any pitch inside the twine rectangle. To improve my hitting, Dad pitched corncobs at me. Anyone who has ever tried to hit a corncob knows you might as well try to hit a bumblebee in a hurricane. After corncobs, baseballs looked like watermelons begging to be busted into pieces. The rest of our city block? We had pigs, with the occasional goat. Wasted, if you ask me.

I wanted to be a major league baseball player—until the day that Dad, a relic of a man, forty-six years old, challenged me to a race to first base. Silly old man. Me in my Rawlings Fleetfoot spikes, him with a No. 2 pencil tucked behind his ear and wearing thick-soled carpenter work shoes that he called clodhoppers. That he beat me in that race by a step was all the reason a teenager needed to tell his father a flat-out lie, which was, "I'll try the next time." There'd be no next time. Losing a footrace to an old man suggested I was overdreaming on baseball. The dream ended forever the first time I saw a ninety-mile-per-hour fastball. I became a sportswriter.

They were always together, Mom and Dad. He had come home from World War II in 1945. By 1949, he was coaching my baseball teams. He drove that pickup, with Mom riding shotgun, to corn towns all over central Illinois to see their son get dirty at shortstop. Once, after a Little League game, someone asked, "Who's your coach?"

I said, "Mr. Smith," or some such.

Mom took me aside. "David, your daddy is the assistant coach. Why didn't you say something about him?"

I had taken Dad for granted. He was always there. Only later, much later, did I learn that some fathers were never there.

Come winter, it was basketball. Dad built a goal in the backyard, a tower of four-by-sixes nailed together to hold a hoop. He also built a trophy case for the high school's Atlanta Redwings, using a jigsaw to carve a wooden "A" with wings painted red. A half-century later, that "A" is in our town's museum.

In the fall of 1963, Dad complained of stomach pain. It had been twelve years since doctors in Chicago removed a cancerous lump from his chin. He was thirty-nine years old at the time of the surgery. Doctors told him to come back every six months for an examination. They also told him to quit smoking because smoking causes cancer. Six years later, on June 12, 1957, the US Surgeon General, Leroy E. Burney, declared it the official position of the

US Public Health Service that a causal relationship between smoking and lung cancer was supported by the evidence. My father, who had smoked since childhood, did not stop smoking. (Most likely, because of the cigarette manufacturer's purposeful addition of addicting nicotine, he could not stop smoking.) He never returned to Chicago for another examination.

In October of '63, doctors did a biopsy of a mass in his stomach. It was a malignant tumor. They told him he might live six weeks.

Mom called a family meeting, meaning her, me, and Sandra.

"Dad thinks he should go somewhere else," she said.

Somewhere else to die, not at home, not with us.

"We're going to have a family vote," she said, "and his vote doesn't count."

The vote was 3–0 for Dad staying where he belonged.

He was at home, dying of lung cancer that had metastasized throughout his body, when he said, "It has been a good year." He had quit school after the eighth grade to work with his father in a sawmill; now he was proud that I had graduated from college that summer. Gussied up in his funerals-and-weddings suit, Dad had boiled in the midday sun during the Illinois Wesleyan University commencement. Cheryl and I also had given him a grandson. When Sandra and Jim Litwiller married in June, Dad put on that suit again to walk her to the altar. "Everything I've always wanted for you kids has happened now," he said.

I didn't know what to say to him. We had never talked much. Dad was fifty-one, I was twenty-two, and we had lived together without knowing each other. He came from a generation of silent men who left school to work through the Depression and left their families to fight a world war. I was a kid who could read and write but had not learned to talk. I had been running for four years—to school and baseball fields, to work, and home to my wife and son. Now Dad was dying, and I wanted to help him. I wanted him to know I loved him. I didn't know if he knew that.

One night he sat at the kitchen table, silent. Finally, I put a hand on his shoulder. I said, "I'll teach my son everything you taught me about baseball." I didn't know how to say I loved him. That was as close as I could come. We shared baseball.

"No," he said. "You teach him everything you know. You know more than I ever did." That was as close as he could come.

After the biopsy, Dad started a woodworking project. For years he had made muzzle-loading guns; his latest was a pistol with a walnut stock. He wanted to hang the pistol in a frame. He would leave the house for an hour at a time and go to an old shed where he kept his saws and miter boxes. He chose walnut for the frame as well, a lighter shade that allowed the pistol the prominence it deserved. He cut the four pieces of the frame to fit so precisely as to make their seams invisible.

Only one thing was left undone.

Before he could finish the frame—he planned a back panel covered in green velvet—he grew weak and was admitted to a hospital.

"You can put the back on someday," he told me.

On Sunday, November 10, 1963, Dad left the hospital to go to one last turkey shoot. He had formed a club of shooters who used the muzzle-loading rifles of a century past. He rested on a gurney in an ambulance. As we came over the hills and headed toward the pasture alongside a country creek where his friends had set up the day's targets, we could hear an occasional shot ring out. The sound made Dad smile.

He wore his familiar black cowboy hat with a pheasant feather in the band, and when they lifted him out of the ambulance on the gurney, he asked someone to prop him up so he could see. Silent all the way to the range, once there he laughed and talked with the shooters. Someone asked for a picture. A group picture. Everyone. Family and friends. Twenty-two people gathered around him. He sat on the gurney, smiling.

Everyone was in the picture except me. I refused. Mom asked me to get beside her. Sandra asked me. For reasons unknown then and little more known now, I would not get in that group photograph with my dying father.

Years later, I asked a psychiatrist why I refused.

He said, "Were you angry?"

I suppose so, though I had no way to say it. Only later did I understand that I might be angry at having missed his life. He was sixteen when his father died of a heart attack. He left school to work and help his mother raise his three sisters. He enlisted in the Army at age twenty-nine and arrived on Omaha Beach thirteen days after D-Day. The next winter he was fifty miles from the Battle of the Bulge, stationed in Namur, Belgium, his battalion at risk if the Germans broke through at Bastogne and marched north to the North Sea. He was an old, decrepit man and I was a fleet-footed teenager when he beat me in that race to first base. (Only later did I find his blue ribbons from the 1926 Logan County track meet.) I wished I had said, "Tell me about all of that, Dad, and how you met Mom at Grandma's restaurant, the Midway, and tell me what it was like at Omaha Beach. Tell me."

Yes, I was angry. I wanted to know him. I was angry. I hated cigarettes and I hated cancer and I hated a God who would let my father die. I stayed out of the group picture, even when Dad waved me in. That happened more than fifty years ago, and there is still nothing I regret more than that moment when childish, petulant self-indulgence stole from me a chance to be with my father when it meant the most to him.

There is only one thing I could have been thinking.

It would be a picture of his death, and why should I be in a picture certifying his death, approving it, even celebrating it?

If I stayed out of the picture, my refusal would be a vote to keep him alive, in our house, with us.

Now I know that the day at the turkey shoot was a celebration of a man's life. But on that day, celebration made no sense. No one close to me had ever died. I was confused. On that day in a pasture along a country creek, I was sad and angry. Maybe I refused to get in the picture out of a fear of emotions I'd never felt, a fear that I'd break down. That day I could not have said why I refused to get in the picture, I just did. I stood off to the side, stock-still, shaking my head no, no, I'm staying over here, go ahead.

I look at that picture now. Dad is sitting on the gurney, propped up, his black hat set at a jaunty angle. There's a blanket over his legs. Crouched in the shadows against his right shoulder is Sandy. Directly behind him, Mom. He is surrounded by people who love him, and he is dying and he is smiling. Smiling. Three days later, he died. On this day, he is smiling.

I kept the pistol he made, and it hangs from two rawhide strips in its walnut frame. It has been more than fifty years now, and I still have not added a back panel covered with green velvet. I like to think Dad will come in from the shed and finish it himself.

ooooo

Mom's time came near on Monday, April 7, 2014. I was in Augusta, Georgia, for the Masters. Sandy called to say that our mother, on morphine, was nonresponsive. I began the long drive home and arrived at the nursing home in Morton around midnight.

I sat on the edge of her bed. She was curled onto her left side, asleep. I could hear the gentle hiss of oxygen flowing through tubes into her nose. Her breathing was slow and shallow. I thought of what she had said: "When I'm old enough to die, I'll die." I kissed her forehead. I whispered into her ear, "Thank you, Mom, for being you. I love you." She died the next morning.

I stood by Mom's casket in an Atlanta funeral home and told her friends and family, "I was last in this room fifty years ago, for my dad's funeral." That day, as on the day of the turkey shoot, I was there and not there, present while being absent, a better observer than a son. But a lifetime later, I stood and spoke for Mom.

I said, "Dad died when I was twenty-two and I knew nothing about life, and only now do I know the most important thing—that I was loved no matter what. Mom's and Dad's greatest gift to me, and a gift that I continue to receive, and that my sister, Sandra, receives was—I didn't have a name for it fifty years ago, but I now know it was unconditional love."

I held a notebook of Mom's. "Here's her scorekeeping from an Illinois Wesleyan baseball game in Jackson, Tennessee. You'll see 'Dave' batted eighth that day. He walked, got hit by a pitch, and popped up to second. The extraordinary thing about the notebook is not that Mom had learned to keep score—did I teach her or did she teach me? The extraordinary thing was not that she was in Tennessee in March for a baseball game or that she and Dad had driven four hundred miles to see their kid pop up and make an error. 'E4' is in the notebook too. The extraordinary thing is that Mom and Dad did *all* those things. It was years later before I learned that some parents do none of those things."

I read from a paper written by our great-niece Jessi Menold as part of a school project. She interviewed Mom when she was ninety years old. Mom said, "I enjoy life at ninety because I've got my kids, my grandkids, my family. A lot of people don't have that, but I still got it. I'll always be thankful. I wouldn't change a darn thing."

There by the casket, I said, "Neither would we, Mom, neither would we. We love you. God bless you."

FOURTEEN

As they worked together in North Carolina's freezing early months of 2013, Butch, the carpenter, heard Jared's stories. He heard about an El Salvadoran who walked into a river, and he heard about prickly pears in the desert and nights sleeping on a Mississippi River wharf. The carpenter heard his helper's stories and he knew, before anyone else, that Jared wasn't long for Mount Airy. Butch said, "The stories he told, the way he told 'em, he had a young man's wanderlust in him. He didn't like to sit still. He'd had enough of that with us."

Maggie's mother knew it too. "As spring came," Kayla said, "you could see Jared was getting itchy." But she thought his restlessness had nothing much to do with sitting still. She believed Jared knew the cost he would have to pay if he quit the road. "I think getting hit by that car in Arizona altered his own self-concept so much that he was so broken, inside and out. And he was not willing to make the effort to settle down." Kayla knew that meant a return to drinking, and that meant more than splitting a forty-ounce beer once a week. It meant a river of vodka. Kayla said, "I told Jared, 'You're going to die way too young,' and he'd go, 'Probably,' and change the subject."

Maggie wanted a life with Jared, and if it couldn't be a life with a place of their own, a life so ordinary as to be wonderful, then she would settle for a life on the road with him—but no, no, it would not be a life that took them where she knew Jared wanted to go. She would not go to New Orleans. Too much booze, too many Scurvy Bastards on the wharf, too much danger in the derelict squats. Maggie gave Jared a choice, "It's New Orleans or me."

Happily, if slowly, he had learned the dangerous lessons of New Orleans. He agreed on an itinerary that took them north out of Mount Airy, away from NOLA.

The morning of Mother's Day, May 13, 2013, Jared finished planting an herb garden alongside Kayla's front porch. Then she drove Maggie and Jared halfway to Asheville. There they caught a ride with a traveling friend, Tammy.

And they were gone.

Jared left behind the golden kitten that had come to him on Kayla's porch. "Spud always made me happy," Kayla said. "I felt Jared's spirit in that little cat." Spud slept on a high shelf in Kayla's bedroom closet, as close to the attic room as he could get.

Three weeks later, Jared called me.

"We're back on the road," he said.

"What? Where are you, boy?" I said.

Life's a blur when you're hopping trains and you're back to drinking half-gallons and you're not sure where you are or where you're going, you just know you've moved through Asheville and Johnson City, Tennessee, and Westville, Ohio, and you've come to a nighttime stop in a big yard that you remember is . . .

"Hagerstown."

They were in Hagerstown, Maryland, three weeks out of Mount Airy, three weeks since Kayla kissed him goodbye.

"I had another seizure here, had to go to a hospital," he said.

"Damn, boy."

"Maggie says she'll kick my ass if it happens again," he said.

I said, "Good for Maggie."

Jared laughed and repeated the words to Maggie, and I heard her voice in the background, a shouted voice, "Fuck yeah, I'll kick your ass good."

I asked when we might see him again. It had been too long. Cheryl and I had left Virginia for Illinois three years earlier. In the time before train-hopping, he occasionally came by our house in the country, usually with his buddy Dear God, just to say hi, and then he'd be off for another adventure. At least once, Dear God persuaded Jared to fire up my big John Deere tractor to go two miles down a country road to a convenience store for a six-pack of beer. Now, never really sure where he was and certainly unsure of where he would be, Jared said, "I'm trying, Grandpa, to get down your way."

"Jared, we're not 'down' any way now," I said. "We're in Illinois. Get yourself to Chicago sometime, I'll find you." And I said, "Be safe, take care. I want you to be an old man someday. Love you, boy."

"We will, Grandpa," he said. "See ya later." And he said, "Gotta go, bye."

The phone went silent. I'd come too close to what he didn't want to talk about, that stuff about take care and get old someday. When he had nothing to say that he wanted his grandfather to hear, he ran silent.

I now understand those silences. I understand why he left Myrtle Beach after being hit by a car, why he switched from yes to no on rehab in Virginia, why he left Mount Airy after a winter idyll with a woman he loved. I now understand that Jared had no choice. Addiction made the choices for him. I understood it best after reading David Sheff's *Clean*. The book includes a chapter entitled "Addicts Aren't Weak, Selfish, or Amoral—They're Ill." Sheff writes:

> Unless you've been there, you can't imagine what it's like to watch helplessly as someone you love descends into addiction. The transformation defies logic—until you understand that your loved one is gravely ill with a brain disease that's debilitating, chronic, progressive, and, if left untreated, often fatal.

FIFTEEN

It was the summer of 2013. A month and two days removed from their attic space above Kayla's bedroom in Mount Airy, Jared and Maggie had hitched a ride in upstate New York with a woman named Suzanne Moore. At a stop along the road, while Maggie slept, Moore walked into a field of flowers with Jared.

"Jared picked flowers for Maggie," Moore said. "He said, 'I know she doesn't like this stupid girly stuff, but she's so pretty and I just want to make her happy.' We walked back to the car, and he laid the flowers in her sleeping hand. It's been so long since I've seen a guy pick flowers for a girl out of a field. That moment made me so happy and gave me so much faith that there were still amazing people in this world. It was just the most romantic and most chivalrous thing."

For travelin' kids, a year on the road is a long time. Uninterrupted by the obligations and duties of a mainstream world, road dogs are at each other's sides most of most days. They fly sign together, hop out together, scrounge in dumpsters together, drink together, and wake up together. They may live in a world apart from most of us, but there is no hiding even there—or perhaps especially not there—from the frictions of a relationship. The summer of 2013 was Jared's fourth year on the road. That was a long, long time to be traveling. By then, danger was an hourly presence in his life. It's hard enough to travel America's freeways and railroads with only guile as a ticket. It's harder yet when moving under the influence of alcohol.

One day in Ithaca, shortly after they left Suzanne Moore, Jared saw in Maggie what she had seen in him too many times.

Maggie had taken her dog, Dixie, to a veterinary clinic. In an examining room, waiting for the doctor, Maggie felt dizzy and had hot flashes followed by cold chills. Next thing she knew, she woke up as EMTs were lifting her onto a gurney.

Jared brought liquor to the hospital, cinnamon whiskey with Mountain Dew to chase it. No, no, a nurse said, her blood-alcohol level is still way too high. Jared said she hadn't had a drink all day. That's when he learned that the liver processes an ounce of alcohol an hour. A half-gallon is sixty-four ounces. Her liver was still awash in alcohol from the day before. Maggie said she saw Jared at her bedside "freaking out." He couldn't handle it. Her seizure and hospitalization reminded him of his own DTs, detoxings, and terrors in the night. After that day, they became "picky with each other" and decided to find their way separately into New York City.

They were to meet at their usual spot, a churchyard near Tompkins Square Park in the middle of the East Village on the Lower East Side.

Maggie arrived an hour early, feeling good about it. In five days apart, she had missed Jared and was eager to fix whatever was wrong. But Jared didn't show. He wasn't there at 9:00 p.m., as agreed, not at 10:00, and not after that. Nor did he answer his phone. In the previous two days and again that night, she had sent these six text messages without a reply:

> I'm talking to Tiger. She said yer gonna be in nyc tomorrow so ill be in boston tomorrow and I can get a cheap chinatown to nyc. Please baby. I went on another angry rough patch but I love you and wanna get back together. I thought a lot about it and I cant not be with you. Sorry I was bitchy. Be safe. Sleep good and I really hope to see you soon.

> Im coming to new york to meet back with you. I miss u.

> I'm at the spot. 2d ave and 10th.

> Jared!!! It's Maggie please call me.

> Goblin where the fuck r u?

> My phone is gonna die so I guess Ill see ya round. I've been here for two hours waiting. Wtf!!! I love you. Charge yer damn phone.

Finally, she walked into Tompkins Square Park. There she saw wanderers she knew. She asked if they had seen Goblin.

Yeah, one said. Seen him with Bird.

She knew Bird, a pretty girl.

Bird knew Jared from the year before. They had met in New Orleans in the French Quarter. He had returned from Myrtle Beach on a walking stick, the "hobblin' Goblin" of Sarafina Scarlet's memory. Bird thought he was "so sweet and funny." They stayed together at a squat called the Pink House.

Bird said, "One night we were walking to the Jax Brewery to sleep, and some random dude bro said loudly to me, 'I'll give you twenty bucks to see your tits,' and Goblin went off on him for it."

Jared and Bird had been together in New Orleans only a short time before she rode to Savannah and on to New York City. When Jared showed up in New York in that summer of 2013, he had not seen Bird in over two years. She knew nothing about his time in Mount Airy with Maggie. To Bird, he was the same old Goblin. They shared vodka and they shared the night.

Maggie found Jared with Bird in Tompkins Square the next morning and asked what the hell.

Bird told Maggie, "I didn't know you guys were dating." Then Bird turned to Jared. "Go ahead," she said, "tell Maggie what happened with us."

He had no answer for Maggie, only that he didn't know why he'd done it. Maggie saw vodka half-gallons, empty, and she said, "We'd been doing so good without it. Staying on beer and wine. Five days and you're back in it. Damn, dude."

He cried. He said he was sorry. Sorry about Bird, the vodka, sorry about not meeting up. He said, "I fucked up really bad."

ooooo

They came to an uneasy peace there in Tompkins Square, but Maggie was frightened. She saw darkness ahead. "Someday you're going to be on a train and have a seizure," she said. "Then what the hell are you going to do? You'll fall under the train and get ground up, that's what." She didn't have to ask what would happen if, in his sleep, he had a seizure and rolled down a concrete slope under a bridge onto a freeway. She knew the answer to that because it had already happened.

From New York, they had hopped out on a train to Virginia. Near the squat Jared once shared with Michael Stephen, Jared suffered a seizure under a freeway bridge. He woke up with paramedics over him. He had tumbled downhill until he cracked his head on a sidewalk. Maggie wanted him taken to a hospital, but the medics said he was okay. She knew better. Without alcohol, she knew one seizure would lead to another.

"I told them, 'You might as well come back in an hour, he's going to have another one,'" she said. "It turned out to be forty-five minutes. We were on the Metro subway. They stopped the train and took him off to a hospital. Mike Stephen came to the hospital too, and we took turns sitting on the bed with Jared."

Stephen believed God had sent Jared to repair his broken life in the darkness of an Alexandria squat. He also believed he had unfairly repaid that kindness by so glorifying life on the street that the kid one-upped him and hopped freight trains around America. Stephen wanted redemption, and he wanted Jared to know peace.

MICHAEL'S STORY

Hundreds of times I tried to get to the deep stuff from Jared's childhood. His catchphrase was "I don't want to talk about it." Who knows why these things happen? What was the psychological pain that he had to self-medicate with vodka? Jared never talked about his childhood. He would become defensive.

Not one day went by when I didn't wonder what would have happened to Jared if, instead of me being so caught up in my own pain and my own bullshit, I had stopped even for one second to think, Here is an impressionable eighteen-, nineteen-year-old kid who really looks up to me. He stayed by my side for months. Didn't visit any of his friends. Just me and him day and night. What if, instead of filling his mind with the "romance" of being a fuck-up, I had preached the gospel? Or talked about plans to go to school? If we had spent our time praying instead of me drinking away my pain and letting him drink? What if I had taught him the future was going to be better? That we would get out of this? That we could start a band? Do anything we want. I could have taught him to play guitar. Anything. But I didn't say any of that. He saved my life, and I just said this bullshit. And he listened.

I spent three years trying to undo the damage I did. I wanted to drag him to detox. He always said he just didn't care, that he wasn't going to live to be forty, so why do it? The truth is, he cared too much. He just didn't think he could get through detox.

He called me once and said he'd had a "strange dream." He sold his memories to spirits for gold and silver coins. He said it didn't make sense. Why would anyone sell his memories? I said, "Jared, don't you understand? The coins in the dream are the coins you collect on the street. The 'spirits' are the spirits you drink, rum, whiskey, vodka. You have been selling your memories to those spirits all along. This is your life! I think the dream is telling you to keep your memories for yourself. Don't sell them to those demon spirits."

He was like, "Huh? What do you mean?" Before I could explain it again, he said his famous catch line, "I don't wanna talk about it anymore." Anytime the subject got around to his drinking, he was a brick wall.

I had visited him in the hospital maybe a year before this one. He'd gone in that time with a 0.43 blood-alcohol level. He had the worst case of DTs I'd ever seen. It was a seven-day detox, and on the seventh day he was still blowing numbers and shaking. At one point, he tried to drink his urine. His sick brain thought it had alcohol in it.

This time, like that time, he was just not the Jared who I had thought of as my brother. I brought him a cross, prayer beads, and the New Testament. Just hoping there was a spark of faith in him, that in his desperation he might cling to a spark of the light, that he didn't necessarily need to have faith in some mystical character that died two thousand or eight hundred or five thousand years ago, or some man in the sky with a white beard and flowing robe. The God he needed, the faith he needed, was in himself. And I don't think he had that. Life was a fucked-up struggle for everybody, and he figured that if normal people struggled with it, how was he going to do it?

So I laid the things on his lap. He looked at them, all confused, and he said, "What are those?" I said, "I thought you may want to try to talk to God about your life while you're laid up."

He picked up the beads like they were something filthy and dropped them onto the bedside table. "No, thank you, no," he said. I said, "Why not?" and he snapped, "Look, what's up? Do you want something?"

I said, "Yeah, Jared, I want to bring you some stuff. I brought a pack of new socks and a pair of Carhartt bibs. And some money. I sat it over there by the window."

He didn't even look and didn't say thanks. I knew it wasn't his fault. The alcohol had such a hold on him.

Maggie was heartbroken. She told me she had been in hospitals three times herself, trying to keep up with him. She was heartbroken and scared.

ooooo

In her year with him, Maggie had taken Jared to eight hospitals. This was the first since Mount Airy and Winston-Salem; that time, in December of 2012, she had refused to let him die. "The drive from Houston to home, that's when I knew I loved him," she said. And she knew he loved her that winter in Mount Airy "because who else loves to walk with me and Dixie to the Red Barn?"

Now, late in June of 2013, in the northern Virginia hospital, she asked Stephen to watch Dixie while she went in to see Jared.

"I told Jared, 'I can't do this anymore,'" she said. "'I'm going home. We'll get together later.'"

Maggie was going home, leaving him behind. She had never left him before, and it hurt. She did it because she was frightened by what she had seen and by what she saw coming.

She left by bus for North Carolina, to her mother's place, and she could do that only because Jared had brought Maggie and Kayla together. So long separated, they had become mother and daughter again through him, partners on that drive from Texas to Mount Airy, partners with him through a winter in that little house down the hill from the Red Barn.

For the next six months of 2013 and into the first days of 2014, Maggie and Jared often talked by phone. They made plans to meet up again.

ooooo

On July 9, 2013, Jared called me. He needed $19 for a bus ticket from Amherst, Massachusetts, to New York.

I promised to send the money by Western Union. I also said, again, "We want to see you. Do you go to Chicago at all?"

"I don't know," he said. "I'll let you know."

I didn't expect an answer. It's not as if he operated on Amtrak's schedule.

"What're you doing in New York?" I said. "Meeting Maggie?"

"We broke up," he said.

"Oh. Too bad."

"Just arguing too much. Life on the road. She wants to do her thing. I'll do mine."

That day I knew Maggie only as the name of his latest girlfriend. Now I know more. I now know that what Jared said that day was the least he could have said. He could have told me that Maggie was important to him in ways that no one else ever was. She had saved his life, more than once, and she had taken him into her home. He could have said that by sleeping with her in that attic room above her mother's bedroom he had seen the possibilities of a life off the road. He had fallen in love with a girl who loved him as he was and who was willing, even eager, to be with him forever. How I wish he had told me that. If only he had said that now he wanted to become an old man like his grandpa—had he said any of that, all of us, Cheryl and I and Jeff and Lynn and Lisa and Jacob, would have gone to war together against the life killing him.

Instead, he said only, "We broke up," and I said only, "Oh. Too bad."

I said nothing when I should have said everything. As Jared and Jacob grew up, I had hoped they would trust me with their fears and dreams. Maybe I hoped for more than any grandsons could deliver, or any son, for I had been silent in my father's presence and my son had been silent in my presence. Still, how I wish that Jared, in distress, could have talked to me. How I wish he could have said what frightened him instead of saying, "She wants to do her thing. I'll do mine."

I am a reporter. I ask questions for a living. For fifty years, I have asked questions that helped people tell their stories when they didn't know they had a story to tell. And now, with my grandson's life changing, I asked nothing, not a single damned question. I said only, "Oh. Too bad." Now I know how much Jared could have said that day. Now I know how much he hid, how much he must have hurt. Now I hurt for all those questions unasked and fears unspoken.

SIXTEEN

By that summer of 2013, Cheryl and I had not seen Jared in three years. We last saw him as we were packing up our house before moving from Virginia to Illinois. In those missing years, the Jared we knew was a voice on the phone. "Just maxin' and relaxin' and payin' no taxes," he said. He would call with a report on his latest movements, his voice chirpy, his tone that of a kid having fun, even when a bodybuilding friend had cajoled him into workouts that left him breathless. "Sixty-five push-ups every day," Jared said. "And we're doing Tysons too."

A sportswriting grandfather knew about physical workouts, and I had seen Mike Tyson first win boxing's heavyweight championship. Yet I knew nothing of "Tysons." Jared said, "It's a prison thing. Tyson did 'em. You take a deck of cards and put 'em on the floor. Then you squat down, all the way down, and pick up a card with your butt crack, and straighten up. You squat again until you've picked up all the cards."

The image was disconcerting enough, let alone the thought of performing the trick. "I won't be doing those," I said.

We hoped he would soon be back with Maggie. On Facebook we had seen a picture of them, a boy and a girl having fun, smiling amid rubble next to the shining steel stripes of a railroad track. They held a case of beer as if it were a trophy for Best-Looking Couple Out There. I knew how proud he was of his porch-building work with Butch in Mount Airy. Maybe they'd be together in Carolina again.

"Where are you now, boy?" I asked.

"We're in Jacksonville, Florida."

"Who's 'we'?"

"Me, Jimbo, and Aggro."

"Aggro? Who's that? What kind of name is that?"

"She's a girl. Aggro—short for aggressive and aggravating."

Discharging himself AMA from the Virginia hospital after Maggie left town, Jared had hitchhiked to Baltimore. There he hooked up with Craig AntiHero, the neophyte tattoo artist who had done his face with a powered-up toothbrush. Along the way, they met Jimbo and Aggro, traveling together as a couple (and once arrested in Fredericksburg, Virginia, for "public indecency," the legal term of art for sexual intercourse practiced on grass behind a grocery store). Aggro, whose given name was Charity Ann Williams, was twenty-eight years old. She'd been on the road nine years. With five or six phone calls, she said, she could find anybody out there. As it happened, she and Jimbo knew people Jared knew, and he knew people they knew. They became an instant new crew: Goblin, Jimbo, and Aggro.

Perhaps Jared recognized the name Aggro. He had heard it months before, during his Mount Airy idyll. The grapevine rumor had someone named Aggro and guys named Eddo and Jewls beating up a kid in California and leaving him for dead. If Jared made the connection between his new pal and that incident, he didn't let on. Out there, you hear about a lot of people dying.

Aggro, Jimbo, and Jared had gone south to Jacksonville and now would ride north to Myrtle Beach.

"Then we'll shoot up to Dad's for the Chili Cook-Off," Jared said.

The cook-off was a family friend's annual October outing.

I said, "Really? You'll be at the cook-off? We'll be there then too."

How wonderful that by the happiest of coincidences we could be with Jared again. For the first time, we would meet him in both his roles, as our grandson and as a travelin' kid, twenty-four years old, a young man on that journey I wrote about the week of his birth, a journey "full of hope and peril, sadness and joy."

That day I would hear Aggro's account of first meeting Jared in front of a gas station next to a liquor store. She said, "After two thirty racks," meaning two thirty-can cases of beer, Craig Anti-Hero tried to steal two half-gallons of Jack Daniel's. "That ended up with the sales clerk chasing him out of the store and beating on him in the street. Seeing this, Goblin ran out into that busy street to save Craig and got hit by a car, not bad, just enough to knock him off stride. Later I found out he'd been really hit by a car in Arizona. That's when I knew he was good people. I mean, if you've already been run down once and you're still crazy enough to bounce through cars to help your friend in a fight, I want you on my team."

Aggro's Story

From the Baltimore hop-out where we met Goblin, we figured we were going to ride through DC and, considering the security there, we needed a good ride to hide in. An empty gondola was our best choice. But once we got to the outskirts, an Amtrak conductor spotted us and called in to the authorities. So we got pulled off by a CSX engineer.

He said Amtrak wanted him to call the police on us, but he wouldn't do that. He told us, "I don't give a fuck. And CSX doesn't give a shit." So, being a nice guy, he walked us to the last locomotive, the fifth unit in the string, and said we could ride there. After that dirty, hot gondola, this was like riding in a Cadillac. He gave us each a cigarette and turned on the air-conditioning and told us he could drop us in Richmond. That was Goblin's first ride ever in a locomotive, and he was thrilled. The CSX guy said, "Enjoy yourselves. And don't touch any buttons!"

One of them, Jimbo or Goblin, ended up hitting the bell button anyway.

Later, trying to hop out at Rocky Mount, North Carolina, we saw a train being refueled, and Jimbo asked the engineer about his destination. The engineer yelled to him, "Might be going to Hamlet, might be going to Florence, might be going to Jacksonville. I don't know, I just drive the thing. But I do know it's going south."

The three of us stood there, looked at one another, shrugged, and said, "Fuck it, we're going somewhere."

○○○○○

Aggro was an old-timer in the dirty, thrilling, complex, dangerous world of train-hoppers. She knew it all. Later, I asked her questions, and she wrote me long letters printed neatly on yellow legal-pad paper, such as this:

The first thing everybody says when they find out I ride trains is, "Oh my God, people still do that?" Yes, a lot. "Oh my God, how do you do that?" I tell them there's no way a completely sane person can live the way we do and enjoy it. We're all a little crazy. What kind of person willingly and happily gives up their home, all their possessions, and sometimes their family, to live in the streets? For some of us, being on the street was better than home. Some people don't choose to be home-less, but all train riders chose trains. I've yet to meet someone who was scary crazy, and I don't think I've ever come across any psychos. But how would I know? We all thought alike.

Anyone can look at a dirty kid in Carhartts with a backpack and/or dog and think "hobo," just like anyone can look at a beagle and think "dog." But a beagle is not a Saint Bernard, just as all 'boes are not cut from the same cloth. We've got junkies and alkies (alcoholics), coffee snobs and vegans, oogles and elitists. Everyone fits into their own tribe. There are even some hippies among us! Oogles are the ignorant young kids that have just started out and know dick about freight trains, usually impres-sionable little shits, to be honest. Elitists are what we call "train nerds" or "train core." They think they know the rails like they built them. They do know stuff, so they're not so bad if you can put up with the attitude. That's why we separate ourselves into different sects, divided up into crews, like Goblin's "Scurvy Bastards." Not all of us can get along. . . .

We're primal people. Don't get me wrong, some of the most well-educated and well-read people I've met are among the hoboes, but we live by the law of the wild. Everything is body language and pheromones. Yes, pheromones. No deodorant for this crowd.

There's no one leader. All of us are running from or shunning the authority of a society that we either don't understand or don't want to understand. That includes authority figures, thus the dislike of religion, politics, all law enforcement—with the exception of the Secret Service, they're pretty cool. Like any pack of ferals, we fall in line to a dominant personality. Dominance by brute strength and intimidation or domi-nance by sly persuasion. But it's not all jungle yodeling and chest pound-ing. An "alpha" has to think like one too. He or she is responsible for the whole pack. . . .

There are some old-timers out there we call "gearless and fearless" because they travel with nothing but the clothes on their back and a small *day-pack for food. They're the best, the troubadours of the rails. You can learn a lot from those guys. I know it sounds strange, but for some of us they're the only father figures we've ever had. The same goes for the older female riders—though they're mostly retired by the time they hit the age to have "Mama" attached to their names. We've got more brothers and sisters than we could ever possibly count. Ranging from crazy-ass punk-rock kids with face tattoos and piercings to old-timey-style-dressed elitists with felt brimmed hats and suspenders. Put it all together and it shows the evolution of an idea into a culture into a whole other society. It's an underbelly of America that most people don't even know exists. . . .*

ooooo

Yes, those underbelly people stink. They smell of grease and mud and bodily fluids; it's not like there are public showers along railroad tracks, which means the body odors of the seriously unwashed become next to palpable. Aggro rule of the road #1: Don't trust a tramp who smells like soap. Rule #2: If they wear cologne, run 'em out of camp. "All of us think that shit stinks."

ooooo

There's a sisterhood of lady riders—and it sure as hell doesn't include what we call "squat mattresses." A squat mattress is exactly what it sounds like—a female who'll let any guy sleep on her. Not classified as a "slut"—sluts are not looked down on in our world. But, excuse my language, squat mattresses are cum dumpsters. Many train ladies will proudly call themselves sluts or whores. Sluts do it for the love of sex, whores do it to get what they want. Squat mattresses do it because they think it's cute and will get guys to like them. They are despised by us lady riders who would never lower ourselves to that level. Our motto is, if you don't like us, there must be something wrong with you. . . .

*We do have characters, from complete sweethearts like Goblin to se-
rious hard-asses. One comes to mind. He was a lean, mean, destroying
machine. Looked like John Henry personified. His hands were the size of
my face, one fist like two of mine, not a kid to be messed with. One time
he almost ripped a kid's ear off. Bunch of high school kids coming out of a
hotel. Prom or something. This guy bumped into one of them and apol-
ogized. The kid scoffs and turns away. BIG MISTAKE. He took the
kid by the ears to head-butt him—only one ear came off. It was hanging
from a little piece of skin. He looked at it, tried to put it back, and when
it wouldn't go back on, we all took off.*

*How many people do I know in the train tramp tribe? Couple
hundred, maybe more. The longer you ride, the fewer people you know.
When someone starts out, they don't know anyone and it's one big ex-
citing adventure full of possibilities and intriguing people, some of them
terrifying. By the time you hit your intermediate years, you know quite
a few people and if you don't know them, you will soon. Those years
you're riding hard and not making plans, just riding for the love of
it. By the end of those years, it seems the kids get younger and all your
friends are settling down, having kids, dying, or already dead. I'm at
the eight-year mark, though that doesn't mean eight straight years riding. Sometimes I take a "vacation" and house-up for a little bit, but I
still count those years. Being inside for a while didn't change my attitude
or outlook on life. I know that I will ride until the day I die. Come
hell or high water, when all is said and done, I'll be on the next thing
smokin', bound for God only knows where. . . .*

○○○○○

I asked, "How do you find trains?" The answer was as simple as
it was unexpected. Sometimes she just went to the public library.
Chicago had a good one. "They've got satellite images of all the
yards." She would first spray herself with Febreze—snuffing out a

travelin' kid's odors—and then, with perfect manners and diction, say at a reception desk, "Excuse me, I'm a rail enthusiast. Do you have any maps of the railroads coming into Chicago?" And thank you very much.

ooooo

Next to "suicides," where you can roll through an opening and onto the racks, empty boxcars are the worst places to ride. You're in the rolling thunder of steel doors and steel floors, everything rattling, a "roar best appreciated by fans of Death Metal music." To be on "door watch" means it's your job to "spike" the doors. You jam a railroad spike in a space in the floor so the doors can't slide shut and trap you in there until yard bulls open them and take you to jail, if you've managed to stay alive. Don't ride an empty coal car because they can dump coal on top of you. For that matter, don't ride a loaded coal car. You're on top of the coal, but you can sink in it as if it's quicksand. The ultimate horror is that the bottom sluice gate opens and the coal goes sliding into a great dark abyss and you slide with it. You're next heard from, if ever, when workmen uncover your blackened corpse.

Another popular ride is grainer porches—the small, flat landing on either end of a grain car. But they often have as much open space as flooring. On a "suicide porch," if you toss and turn in your sleep, you might roll off the porch and under the train. Getting shaken around on the trains is one of the reasons we say every year on the rails adds an extra one to your actual age.

You asked about religion on the rails. Someone who doesn't know better would say there isn't any. But there is one religion on the rails. If we're having a shitty day panhandling or going to catch out, we all say a silent prayer to the train gods. There's no shape or a look, the way Christians view God. But the train gods live on the great freight in the sky. When you die, old-timers call it "catching that westbound." I'm assuming "west" because that's where the sun sets. You know the song "Big Rock Candy Mountain"? Well, that's what heaven would be like for us. A mama 'bo taught me the rhyme when I was still wet behind the ears. If you're a good 'bo when you die, you go to ride that great freight in the sky. If you're bad, you don't go to hell, you end up in a place much worse than that—you go to North Platte!

Road dogs? Road dogs are family. They're not someone you drink with while you're in town or at a hop-out spot. They're not kids you haven't seen in a while and then hang out with for a week. Road dogs are people you make miles with. They are your brothers-in-arms, your confidants, your running partners, someone whose side you'll take and fight [for] even when they're wrong! I've had only four road dogs—three girls and one guy. Two are dead, one retired, and the other is in a van. The one I rode the longest with was "Coon Head," real name Beth. She was a young kid from San Antonio and didn't know anything. Got suckered into going on the road with a dude she thought she could trust and ended up getting ditched.

My ex-husband—long story—found her in a drinking circle and took a shine to her. Not in that way. He just liked adopting kids. I hung out with her for a few days before deciding I liked her too. We became fast friends, and she was always my road dog before his. She rode with us all through the South, down to Florida and up into Kentucky and Tennessee. I wish we had ditched his ass then and went our own way, maybe we'd still be riding. But she went back home to help out her folks and stayed. We keep in touch, and I'm always asking when she's coming back.

ooooo

If it's not a family out there, it's certainly a fraternity or sorority with expectations. The best way to know who's good and who's not is to invite them to pitch in on booze and drugs—unless, Aggro said, the wannabe is a girl and she's alone "and one of your boys wants to get laid." That gets her into the circle. "Which is really annoying to us sisters."

○○○○○

How do we get along when we're wasted? We get along great! Once again, the key is respect. If you do or say something that someone is offended by, apologize and move on, don't do it again. I've got a saying, "Puppies get schooled." If you keep messing up, we'll let you know. Unlike any other group, we can put away a lot of booze and get really rowdy but still be completely coherent. One second, it's all fun and games. The next second, everyone's looking to kick some ass.

The thing about the train-rider culture is, we take care of our own. A good friend told me that "hobo" stands for Helping Other Brothers Out. Here's my story. When I first hit the rails, my road dog and I came to Sacramento. We raged that town hard. Making out like bandits, acting like land pirates. (Take what you can, and give nothing back!) Then I got sick. My liver started going out on me. I couldn't even get out of my bag to feed and walk my dog. This ol' 'bo I had met the day before heard from my road dog that I was sick. So he came by to check on me. Said I looked like death on a cracker, but he knew I wouldn't go to the hospital on account of my dog. He came by every day, bringing me food, water, and tall cans of PBR so I wouldn't die. He walked and fed my pup too. After a week of me in the bag, the cops showed up and said I had two hours to get moving or they were calling an ambulance. I got up and made a quick eighty bucks. You can do that in downtown Sac if you look like death and you're only twenty years of age. I gave the 'bo the money, he tried to give it back and I told him no. So, he and I proceeded to the booze store and got everyone drunk. That's how it's done out here.

We can be a rather melancholy bunch sometimes. We get depressed and lonely, just like everyone else—although I suspect some of us like it. Feeling pain is sometimes the only way to know you're alive. We handle

*it the same way we handle everything—self-medicate. The most popu-
lar methods being alcohol and other drugs. That's why train kids are so
weird when we're sober. We operate outside of society inebriated for so
long that we forget how to interact with it. Things that would disgust
and horrify a "normal" person, we wouldn't bat an eye at. Our most
proud moments are when we simply walk off the darkness. One thing
about riders: we don't dare show weakness. We don't see tears as weakness, but that's more of a private thing. I can't even force myself to cry in
public. If I can't swallow my pain, I'll ride hard until I can't feel anymore. Some might say that's running from it. I call it therapy.*

*Pain and sorrow are a rider's worst nightmares. They can eat us
alive, and we'll do anything to avoid those feelings, even if it means becoming an alcoholic or a junkie because being sober is so much worse. A
lot of us come from broken homes with fucked-up pasts. We choose this life
because it's the most free and the happiest we've ever felt.*

ooooo

Aggro and her guys wound up in Jacksonville, where cops rousted
them from a street corner because, Jared said, "The white people
were afraid of us, like we're crackheads, just pulling stuff out of
their ass."

The day produced memories. Jared called to tell me: "I saw this
really cute black girl, Grandpa, seriously, she was, like, seven feet
tall. I asked her if she was a basketball player. Nope, a fry cook.
Had tattoos on her arms and face. I liked her." A pause. "I think
she's a lesbian, though."

It was the first of his flirtations that day. "We also ran into this
guy Aggro knows, name's Eddo. He's gay. Apparently, he thought
I was gorgeous. Yep, that's how it works for me. Had a lesbo and a
gay guy after me."

Eddo. Another name from the grapevine.

Cheryl told me later that Jared mentioned two friends who had died that week of drug overdoses.

"You're not doing drugs, are you, Jared?" she asked.

"No, no," he said.

On September 12, up from Jacksonville to Myrtle Beach, Jared walked with his mother at the ocean's edge, near the place where she had asked him what in his life he would want washed away and with his walking stick he had scratched in the sand, BOOZE.

To Aggro, the sight of mother and son at each other's sides was further confirmation that Goblin was "a different dude." She said, "I'm still not sure what it was, but it was like he lived on another plane of existence. He could laugh at whatever life threw him. Like he knew something we all didn't. At Myrtle Beach, I watched him and his mom walk down the beach together. They were looking for shells and shark teeth. For everything else that was going on with him, he was so content at that moment. It was like at that moment nothing else mattered and everything was right with the world in his eyes just because his mother was near him."

Lynn believed he wanted to quit drinking. "No one can tell me he didn't want it," she said. "But the alcohol did what the alcohol wanted to do." That day in September, she offered him a bedroom in her home with the guarantee of a job at a custom-motorcycle shop.

Thanks, he said, but no. He was happy out there.

Lynn said, "Why do you say you're happy, Jared?"

"Everybody else is always worried about money and paying bills and they're never happy, Mom. I'm happy every day. Like today, it's going to be a good day."

"But, Jared, a good day? A good day drinking? You do realize that alcohol will kill you. You do know your pancreas won't get better unless you stop. It will just get worse."

"Mom, c'mon. I don't want to talk about it. I'm cutting down on the vodka."

"Your liver doesn't know the difference, honey, it's all alcohol. One day a seizure will kill you or leave you in a vegetative state."

"Mom," he said.

"One day I know I'm going to get the call. I just know I am. Bottom line, Jared, I gotta know one thing."

She had tried everything else. Now she would try to scare him.

"Do you want to be buried or cremated?"

"Mom! Wow, Mom."

Lynn had failed, as everyone had failed, to talk her son out of his drinking. Now she had moved to a mother's primal scream.

She said, "Yeah, Jared, 'Wow.' Which is it?"

That bright September day the mother gave her son a seashell they'd picked up on the beach. She told him to keep it forever and whenever he put his hand in his Carhartts pocket and felt the seashell, that was her giving him a hug and kiss.

SEVENTEEN

A month later, Cheryl and I drove south out of Washington, DC, and wound our way west and south again through Civil War battlefields to our son's house, a little farm in the scrubby pinewoods outside Orange, Virginia. The next morning we would stand on the same ground as Jeff and Jared, ground where Kindreds from northern England settled three hundred years earlier. We had never seen this Goblin who was Jared. Nor did we know what our son, Jeff, thought of his son, the Jared who became Goblin. The three Kindred men would be together for the first time in four years. The night before that meeting, I sat with Jeff at his kitchen table, and we talked in ways we should have talked years before.

I had gone too long in silence, burning with anger since that phone call from Montana thirteen years earlier. I had become an old man, and it was time, before time ran out, to do a right thing. I had not done right by my father that day of the muzzle-loading shoot, refusing to stand with him for a photograph as he lay dying.

Silence owned me then and owned me in Montana and now, with my son in his home, I would not allow silence to own me still.

I wanted to know how Jeff had come to shout, "*I'm the parent here.*" I still considered those words tormenting reminders of a workaholic father's failures so grievous that a son not only would dismiss the father's advice against splitting up brothers, he would do it with rage in his voice.

"I've felt bad about our phone call ever since," I said.

"Yeah, we sent Jared to Lynn's," Jeff said.

"When you shouted, 'I'm the parent here,' I just hung up on you."

Jeff didn't remember it. "A phone call like that? Nope."

He popped open a beer. He held the can in one hand and popped the top with the thumb of that hand.

A son shouts down his father and forgets it?

Again, as on that Montana night, I said nothing. But a lifetime later the silence hid no anger. I had come to see Jared, not to force open old wounds. I had come for a purpose that I didn't realize until it was happening. I had come to tell my son I was sorry.

"I'm sorry that we had to have that call," I said. "And I want to say I'm sorry that I wasn't a better father for you."

Jeff put down his beer and looked at me.

"What?" he said. "What are you talking about?"

"How I screwed up."

"C'mon, you were a great father."

"I was gone all the time."

"Dad, don't beat yourself up. You did great. I work like I do because you did. The work ethic I have, I got that from you. My job now, the boss is all about family. If you need a day off to be with your family, the boss says take it. And it's stressful for me to even do that. I worked the way I did for one reason. My motto was 'I'm

going to be as good a Ford mechanic as my dad is a sportswriter.'
I still remember all those days you took me with you to the sports
department in Louisville. I wasn't even in school yet and you'd go
in early to try to find a story. You'd set me at a typewriter and give
me some paper. I'd go through your mail and get the *Speed Sport
News*, Chris Economaki's paper about racing. You had me working before kindergarten. The best part, though, was the vending
machine—Cokes and candy."

In high school, my history teacher, Phil McCullough, once
told the class that my father was a hard worker. He said those two
words—"hard worker"—more than a half-century ago and I never
forgot them. It was a small thing from a teacher, an aside in class,
a moment that had nothing to do with teaching history and everything to do with teaching life. Now, at my son's kitchen table, I
heard what I never expected to hear: that what my father taught me
about work I had taught Jeff about work.

"And what other kid gets to do the things I did with you?" Jeff
was on a streak now. "Like that day with the Louisville Cardinals.
That football game, the spring game, where they had you as a ce-
lebrity coach. You took me along, I was maybe six or seven, and we
stood on the sidelines, you coaching and me your assistant."

Really?

"And Daytona. We went to all those 500s. How many kids get
to do that? I sat on a pile of tires in the garage area talking to Richard Petty. I took a piss next to Buddy Baker while Cale Yarbor-
ough was taking a shower in the drivers' room. Ever since, I have
been everybody's go-to NASCAR expert. At school I'd go around
asking my buddies, 'So where's your dad this week? Mine's at the
Super Bowl, goes every year, brings me back stuff.'"

Well . . .

"And the bikes we rode together."

Jeff was ten years old when we bought motorcycles. I'd ridden once, crashed, bummed up a shoulder, wrote a column about it. So while Jeff became a motocross racer, I was happy to ride alone in the woods and hills and gullies, where it was safer for old men.

"Like that day you put Mom on your YZ," Jeff said. "Soon as she kicked it in gear, she ran it up a tree. It was great. You both were great when I was growing up." (Nah, I was bad, totally. Cheryl's very good, excellent day on a motorcycle became the stuff of family-bonding lore. I wrote a comic column about it. Writers write.)

Okay, maybe there were moments. Maybe, in my silent way, I'd done for Jeff what my father, in his silent way, had done for me. I was relieved by Jeff's recall of glad moments a generation old. I was happy that we had ended a long silence that had come between a father and a son. To celebrate, I next said, "Son, can I have one of those beers?"

Now I could ask a storyteller's questions. "Why do you think Jared chose a life on the road?"

"Good question," Jeff said, and he said it in a tone suggesting he had never considered asking such a thing. "I don't know. He just liked having absolutely no responsibility, evidently. That's the only thing I can come up with. That, and being free to do what he wanted to do."

After all of it—the divorce, separating the brothers, Jacob's feeling that they weren't welcome at home after high school and they should go join the Marines—Jeff said he wished he'd done one thing better. "Sometimes I'd be on the phone with Lynn and I was so angry I'd be calling her every filthy name in the book—and the boys would be hearing it all. That's a regret I have. I shouldn't have been doing that."

He also saw one curious thing in Jared's early life.

"He didn't care about getting a driver's license. What sixteen-year-old isn't excited about getting his license? He just didn't care. Like he wanted to stay off the grid. Like he was a nineteenth-century guy and wanted to live in a world where there weren't licenses and taxes and he could just live off the land. A modern-day hobo."

Then this:

"Bottom line," Jeff said, "he liked drinking and being drunk. It's what he liked."

"When, you think, did he start drinking?"

"He must have started doing it when he was a senior in high school. I never knew it, except that time he was seventeen and the sheriff's office brought him home. They said he'd been drunk outside a Food Lion. Also, he might have started five years before that—when he went to live with Lynn in Fairfax. He probably got in all kinds of crap up there before he came back to live with us his senior year."

"You ever talk to Jared about the drinking?"

"Just to tell him he had to stop. He'd done a really good job of hiding it. He did that because he didn't want to be a disappointment to me. I never said anything like, 'You're a worthless loser not going anywhere.' But I do get criticized a lot for my facial expressions. I'm sure I displayed my disappointment that way. But all I ever said to him was 'Jared, you got to stop, you got to slow down. You got to stop the drinking. It's going to kill you.' And he'd say, 'Oh yeah, Dad, I've almost stopped.'"

Leaving I-95 that morning, going to meet them all at Jeff's place, Cheryl and I had driven west on Virginia's Route 3 through Fredericksburg and on another fifteen miles to Locust Grove, nothing more than a dot on the map. Sixteen years earlier, we had bought a house and 175 acres there along a stream called Russell Run. Two hundred yards from our house, we built another house that we sold to Jeff and Lisa. The property was a world unto itself. Down a lane a mile long, everything we could see was ours. The day we moved in, Jared and Jacob were eight years old, bouncing back and forth from their parents' house to ours. Again, as in Newnan, we believed we'd be there forever.

Now Jared was twenty-four. He lived nowhere and everywhere. We knew only a little about his life. We'd heard about Maggie and the speeding car in Arizona and the Michigan doctor's warning. We'd heard that dark stuff. If we didn't dismiss it, we didn't accept it either. Life is hard and you get past the dark stuff and everything turns out good, doesn't it? We were excited about seeing Jeff and eager to see Jared the next day. Jacob was out of town working, but we would be on the little farm with Jeff, Lisa, Kaleb, and Josie. We'd spend a day with Jared and his new road dogs, Jimbo and Aggro.

EIGHTEEN

On the morning of October 19, 2013, Cheryl and I saw Jared. As we drove between tall trees and up a lane, he stood by a garage on his father's little farm. The boy I held on my right hand the first week of his life. The golden child in a white tuxedo and purple cummerbund. The teenage punk in his studded jacket and Mohawk. There he was now, twenty-four years old, a travelin' kid off America's railroads. Waiting for us on Jeff's lane, covered with road grit and grime, a raggedy-ass beard sprouting down from his jawline. And he was by God beautiful.

Beautiful in his travelin' kid uniform. Dirt-smeared Carhartts, the pants too big at the waist, held up by suspenders. Cuffs rolled high above scuffed leather boots, unlaced. A ball cap, with a string woven through it and knotted under his chin so it wouldn't fly off in a train's whirlwind. Around his neck a bandanna, once red and now blackened with oil and grease, the "train rag," as travelin' kids call it, worn unto death or disintegration, whichever came first.

"You never would let me wash those things," Cheryl said to her grandson. She meant the stinking bibs that he had worn living on the street, even before his train-hopping days.

Jared laughed. "Gotta look dirty, or people won't drop any cash on us."

I had feared he would be skin and bones. He was always slight, and I knew the years on the road had been unkind. As we drove from Washington to Orange, there was no reason to imagine he would look as good as he did. Thin, but no thinner than the last time we saw him, he seemed to be strong and healthy, with a touch of rosy color about his face and a light in his eyes. When he came to hug us, he giggled a lot and bounced around, almost dancing, and in the first moments he asked, "Grandpa, do you remember telling me stories about Pee Wee Reese and Muhammad Ali and that soccer guy who kept saying, 'Love, love, love'?"

I had told those stories sixteen years earlier. I had talked him to sleep, a child next to me in bed, listening to the same stories night after night. They were a sportswriter's stories chosen because I knew enough details to fill time until an eight-year-old fell asleep. All that had happened since—life happening—and he still remembered us in bed.

There at his father's home in Virginia I saw Jared as a three-year-old at Newnan's fire station saying, "Bye-bye, fire truck," and sliding under our jukebox looking for Elvis. I could see him, ten years old, swinging in the backyard while his German shepherd, Ikea, ran barking at his flying feet. I could see him, fifteen years old, driving a bouncing, careening go-cart across our pastures. Each day was another miracle made possible by some unknowable biochemical arrangement so complex that we reduce it to one word—life. Those mornings when Jared slept in my bed, I watched him in wonder that such a miracle as that boy could happen. I wanted to protect him, hold him close, keep him safe from a cold, hard, mean world that could, for no reason that made sense, beat him up and leave him lonely. I wanted him to be a kid forever.

There was a tattoo on his left shoulder. SCURVY was written in cursive above a skull with railroad spikes through the eyeholes. Below the skull were the numbers "1 2 3." He explained the markings: "It's 'Scurvy Bastards: Thou shalt not lie, thou shalt not cheat, thou shalt not steal.'" It was a travelin' kid's code of ethics—not the Ten Commandments, but more rules than some ordinary citizens follow and enough to remind me of what Dear God once said of Jared: "So good to everybody, he's a train-hopping Jesus."

Jared's beard. The color of cinnamon. Allowed to grow untended, it was an exotic frame for the blue eyes and fine features of his small face. Later that day we made a family photograph. Smiling, he stood behind his grandmother with his left hand on her left shoulder. His right hand squeezed a tuft of the beard at his chin. "This'll keep me warm all winter," he said.

From Myrtle Beach, Jared, Aggro, and Jimbo had ridden a freight to Richmond, where friends picked them up and drove them north to Orange. "Whenever Jared would come to town," one friend, Sean Lawson, said, "it was like Gandalf from *The Hobbit* had come to visit. He was the great traveler who brought good times and amazing stories. We took to calling him the Nomad. To me he was a symbol of absolute freedom. And I envied his charisma. Man, him and Carlton cigarettes. The really long, skinny ones. He'd say the name like a snob, 'a Caaahhhlton.' And one time he said he'd never drink clear liquor again. He'd punched out a window. But I saw him drinking vodka and called him on it. He said, all high and mighty, 'Not vodka-alcohol, vodka-*water*, fool!' So funny, I gave him a pass."

The better to create distance between civilization and the road dogs' distinctive, long-lasting odors, Jeff had invited/ordered

Jared's crew to stay in his garage. "Got my own *Walking Dead* TV show out there," he said. The star of the show was Charity Ann Williams. "Nobody calls her Charity," Jared said. "She's Aggro."

Unafraid and savvy, thick from shoulders to hips, five foot eight, 170 pounds, tattooed and pierced, Aggro was a dark presence in black boots and black bibs with her scissor-chopped brown hair under a short-billed jeans cap. When she was nineteen and living in Plano, Texas, her high school sweetheart died of a meth overdose. She had been on the road ever since, save for eighteen months when she worked in a San Antonio meatpacking plant. A hard-ass romantic, she practically sang about her first ride on a freight.

"There were four of us riding a flat car between two semi-trailers, otherwise known as a piggyback, from Oakland, California, to Eugene, Oregon. We would hang our feet over the edge, and we'd hide under the axles when passing through towns. It was amazing to ride through the Cascades, surfing the car, seeing the Milky Way in the night sky. I said, 'I'll never hitchhike again.' I fell in love. That first ride, it's like your first kiss, scary but exhilarating at the same time. You know that either you'll ride freight till the day you die or never again. Me, I became married to those steel wheels and miles of track."

During Jared's time with Maggie in Mount Airy—when he first heard Aggro's name, a rider somehow connected to a killing— Aggro spent six months in a Kansas City jail for beating up a "home bum," a vagrant living on the streets of his hometown. On release, she did a Facebook post:

Contrary to popular belief . . . I did NOT do 30 years. I am NOT a heroin addict nor have I ever touched the stuff and I'm out of jail. I'll be staying in Kansas City going to college and learning how to tattoo.

That day in Orange she told me she had learned the source of Jared's good looks. She was sitting on a picnic table when a man walked toward her. "He wore camo slacks and a blue hoodie. I'd never met Jeff, but I looked over at Goblin and said, 'Your dad's here.' One look and I thought, *That's Goblin in twenty years.*"

Twenty years, what a gift that would be. Twenty years from that day, in October of 2033, Jared would be forty-four years old. He'd likely be a husband and father. The handyman work he liked doing with Butch in Mount Airy might be his full-time job; his mother had talked about working in a custom-bike shop because, like his father and like his brother Jacob, he was good with machines.

But twenty years? In twenty years, a wanderer might run through several lives. Aggro's formula was one to five, a year on the road being five at home, meaning Jared's five came to twenty-five. On this second stop of what Aggro called "the Goblin Family Tour," she said, "You better pay attention, we get old quick."

Now Jared sat in Jeff's garage with his second-family siblings. Kaleb was a firefighter in training at age seventeen. Nine-year-old Josie shadowed Jared's every move without ever speaking, eyes wide open to better see this brother she didn't know. She wasn't alone in her curiosity. We had known the Jared who lived in our homes. But the Jared who stood in front of us at his father's farm—I didn't know the travelin' kid Goblin.

I now know he came from San Diego and New Orleans, from upstate New York and the high desert of New Mexico. I know he chased naked girls in an Ocala forest, slept with a French–Puerto Rican beauty on the sands of Coney Island, and found in North Carolina the woman he could have, would have, should have married. "It's fun, Grandpa," he said. And I believed I knew what he meant. He had seen lives in our world that were no fun, that were mean and angry, that were little more sober than his, and he had chosen to live another way.

By the time he arrived at Jeff's place on that day in October of 2013, he had been with street preachers selling Jesus and street urchins selling crack among the mad dogs of Houston's Fifth Ward. He had danced on Bourbon Street and in a gondola moving through the New Mexico night. He had loved the angel-faced singer Sarafina Scarlet. He was an alcoholic and an adventurer, a train-hopping ninja, a leader, lover, and fighter. To quote Maggie again, "He was the happiest guy I'd ever seen."

Jeff's Story

I told him he was the bravest guy I knew. My greatest fear had been that he would be beat to death. I told him, "You're going to get the shit kicked out of you and thrown off a train and never be heard from again. You'll be left somewhere for the coyotes to eat." He'd say, "Naw, not going to happen, Dad."

He knew I was embarrassed by him and wanted him to settle down and get a job. At the same time, I was proud of him. I wouldn't have been able to do what he did. He went farther west than I ever did, he saw more of the country than I ever will. He did what the Civil War campaigners did in the 1860s. They were kids too, a thousand miles from home walking in foreign lands, hopping trains, no way of telling where they were going.

I thought about my great-great-grandfather, Overton Kindred. In his eighties, he'd just take off walking. He'd walk from Illinois to Kentucky, four hundred miles down there, to visit relatives and walk back, nobody knowing where he was. I said, "Jared, you're following kind of a family tradition." I attribute that wanderlust in him to the family genes.

I tried to convince him to be a living historical Civil War campaigner. "Ride a horse across the country, Jared, and you'll get more support than you can imagine." In northern Virginia, there was a guy who rode a horse every year up to Gettysburg along Route 15, the same route the Army of Northern Virginia took. He lived on his horse those two, three weeks. That's why I gave Jared that Confederate slouch hat and eating gear. He'd have been a hero out there.

That part of what he did, I was envious of. He was just like those eighteen-year-old kids in the Civil War—they marched into places where they were scared to death knowing that the next day you'll die. But a faction of them loved it—just the way Jared loved it.

ooooo

Cheryl and I had to leave Orange to get back to Washington early that afternoon. Before leaving, I wanted a photograph of Jared with Robert E. Lee. Orange was the northernmost settlement in the Confederacy from March 1862 to May 1864. In those months, Lee headquartered there. On Jeff's living room wall, there was a handsome print of the general.

I said to Jared, "Let's go take a picture with General Lee."

With a muzzle-loading shotgun in hand, Jared struck a pose in front of the portrait. He raised his chin a click and held the old gun across his chest. To see him then, a skinny kid with a scraggly beard, was to see what Jeff saw, a twenty-first-century version of those young soldiers who marched into places that scared them.

Jared had been to dark places, more even than we knew then, and that afternoon we said our goodbyes to him, to Aggro, and to Jimbo. The three wanderers planned to move on from Virginia to Philadelphia.

"Don't forget, you guys, please stay in touch, someday I want to understand your story," I said. "Tell me why, tell me everything, tell it to me from beginning to the end, don't leave anything out, and make it funny."

Jared: "Oh, yeah, we can make it funny."

Jeff: "Leave out the tragic parts."

Jared: "Yeah, no tragic."

Aggro's Story

The fun parts, okay?—like catching out. Goblin was with us in a little town somewhere near Savannah. We shouldered up our packs after gearing up at the local gas station and headed up to a bridge that crossed the rail yard. You couldn't walk right up to the hop-out on account of a chain-link fence and just plain wilderness. So we hiked up the bridge, legged over the side, dipped down underneath the bridge, and heel-toed our way down an embankment.

At the bottom was a partition about seven feet high. I slipped my backpack straps off my shoulders and let my pack fall with a thud and a cloud of dust. Eyes scanning and searching every beam and surface for a sign in Sharpie ink, paint, chalk, or grease. Symbols, signs, names, and caricatures ranging from elaborate and beautiful to crude stick figures. Saying, like, "Hobo Joe wuz here," signed and dated.

Goblin and I scurry and rummage, tagging here and there where there is space and searching for evidence of a recent hop. Did they leave anything behind? This hop didn't have a firebox, but there was a wood pile and a small grate. The heat coming off the rail yard was tangible. Mixed with the sound of cicadas, it became a creature unto itself. There's a cool dampness under the bridge in the solidified mud and moss. I could smell the rust from the train cars and old tin cans.

There's a break in the trees. What's that over there? We go crunching, snapping, shuffling, crackling through the leaves, twigs, debris. A circle of mismatched dining room chairs, stools, milk crates! Rail tags cover everything! And a wind chime made of glass bottles, pieces of colored glass, rail spikes, pieces of ties, and other hobo mementos.

The tags are Savannah-bound, a couple years old. There's a grate over the pit for cooking. I wished it was cold enough or we were going to be there long enough to use it. Well, damn—"Let's just stay a day," Goblin says with big eyes.

Now it's evening and skeeters are coming with vengeance. All you can smell is Deet, Off, and Deep Woods, and you hear the sound of aerosol spray. Hey, pass the booze! Sodium-vapor lights come to life in the yard like huge stationary fireflies. Automobiles are rumbling over the bridge, train cars creaking and banging around in the yard. The engines hum, tick, and whoop while radios crackle with static and unintelligible voices as the switchmen do what they do best—build our rides.

Smiles in the dark mix with hushed voices and the chuff and snuffle of sleeping dogs. Stories overlap and the laughs get a little bit too loud as the booze lubricates the night. The air smells sweet now, like jasmine and honeysuckle. The sharp taste of straight cheap booze kissed by chaser is on my tongue.

What's that? Did you hear that? A low rumble coming from down the mainline. The night goes from relaxed to supercharged that fast. Now we're sitting up erect, ears twitching, nostrils flared, as if we're the very dogs at our feet. Shhh! Did you hear that? Which way is it coming from? Hurried now, bottle caps are screwed on—shit!—and have to be rethreaded. The rustle and hustle of gear being packed quickly and the shuffling of feet. Ow! Shit! Get the fuck outta the way!

Goblin goes up to the main rail, keeping to the shadows, glancing one way and then the other. There! At the end of the track: a lonesome whistle calls and three lights dance out of the darkness. Watching, waiting.

He steps back down from the track in three quick strides, shufflin' the way he does, taking a pouch of tobacco out of his Carhartts, and all of us are waiting like dogs on a bone. Goblin speaks around the rolled cigarette in his mouth while he sparks the flame, "Northbound!"

ooooo

We had no idea when we would see Jared again. He might have been a soldier home on leave from a war we could not hope to understand. We just wanted him safe, and it was wonderful to see him so happy on this morning at his father's in the woods shimmering with autumn's colors.

It was a day of redemption. The son I loved as best I knew how had brought into his home the son he loved as best he knew how. When he might have stayed away, the son had returned to the father's embrace. What had gone before all those years ago was done, and if not forgotten at least forgiven in ways that made possible a day when we were a family again.

Twenty-one years earlier, Jeff and Lynn had left Georgia with the boys. On that day, Jared, three years old, looked at Cheryl through the window by the van's second-row passenger seat. She saw the sadness of separation on his face. This time, Aggro told me, "Gobs was really emotional about seeing Cheryl. He just was so happy to spend time with her. He talked about this special bond they had."

We stood by Jared at Jeff's garage, and we didn't want to leave, and we stood there some more. We wanted the day to never end. Grandpa hugged him and Grandma hugged him, and we said take care, be safe, if you need anything, call.

"Love you, boy," I said.

"Love you, Grandpa," he said. "Love you, Grandma."

As we drove away, Cheryl saw Jared wave. We were a minute down the road before she spoke.

"Did you see the tears in Jared's eyes?" she said. "He cried when we left, and he tried to not let us know."

ooooo

Two days later, Jeff drove Jared, Aggro, and Jimbo to the Fredericksburg railroad station. The crew planned to head for Philadelphia for Thanksgiving, Christmas, and the New Year's holidays.

"Jared was the first one out of the truck, so excited, he couldn't wait to get out of that truck," Jeff said. "He was getting all their gear out, chattering away, already talking about where they were going, and I'm saying, 'Jared!' Nothing. He's not listening. 'Jared!!' He's doing this, doing that. And Jimbo says, 'Dude! Your dad's trying to get your attention.' Jared goes, 'Oh. Yeah, Dad?'"

Jeff gave him a jacket from his Ford shop and said, "You're going up north, take this."

Jared said, "Cool, Dad. Thanks."

"And off they went," Jeff said. "I didn't know if I'd ever see him again. It was like that every time. Three or four times, he had come to Virginia and stopped to see us. Every time I took him to the train station, I thought it would be the last time I saw him."

NINETEEN

In early December 2013, Jared called from Philadelphia.

"After Christmas," he said, "I'll shoot over to Illinois to see you."

"How will you get here?"

"Freight train," he said.

The logistics of his traveling baffled me then and baffle me yet. I could retrace some of his movements through my notes of phone calls and interviews. But he talked about it casually, as if an illegal, dangerous, 1,500-mile freight train ride from an East Coast metropolis to a stinkweed hamlet in Illinois were nothing more than a sportswriter's commute to a ballpark.

Riding with Jared, Aggro and Jimbo had gone to Philadelphia to pick up a puppy before heading out of the winter's cold, probably to Tennessee. Jared had intended to leave with them, but while helping move furniture for an old acquaintance, he made a new friend—a woman named Brooke. "Jared and I hit it off right away,"

Brooke told me. "He was adorable and funny, just a good-hearted guy who seemed to be enjoying his life."

Instead of going with his pals to Tennessee, Jared decided to stay at Brooke's place in the Kensington neighborhood of Philadelphia. Aggro, who thought of Jared as her little brother, frail and failing, didn't like what she saw happening: "All Jared did for months on the road with me and Jimbo was get sicker and pine away about missing Maggie. He liked Brooke, no doubt, but he told me, 'She's not my Maggie.' He needed help, and here he was dropping us for Brooke."

Brooke's row house stood across from an auto body shop on a crumbling alleyway of a street. The building's brick front was discolored, as if charred by fire or blackened by years of Kensington's gloom. A three-step concrete stoop led to a metal door framed by splintered wood and faded paint. Iron bars crossed the two first-story windows and two basement windows.

A half-mile away, at the intersection of Kensington Avenue and Somerset Street, an elevated train picked up and delivered passengers. The spot was notorious for heroin dealers and prostitutes working the corners, their business seldom interrupted by Philadelphia police more concerned with homicides and gang wars. Brooke's advice: "Don't go there at night."

"That neighborhood never had a lot of people on the streets," Aggro said. "The house had a weird location, kind of on a side street. I wouldn't really say it was a hellhole, but it is an open-air drug market. Those people congregated at the el stops and by food-stamp offices. Mostly, the neighborhood lacked activity. You could feel it in the air, sort of a 'blah' effect, like nothing was going on, no life in it."

Brooke's place had "long, narrow hardwood floors, all of it dirty, like they never cleaned," Aggro said. "There were dog and cat hair balls camped around the baseboards, and her roommate's dog thought the best bathroom was in the corner of the kitchen. The dog wouldn't even ask to be let out, would just go. With the exception of the furniture, you could, at a glance, mistake it for a squat. And no dishes. They had no dishes. I was always wondering how they cooked, until I found out they didn't. Whatever. It was not a place to walk around in barefoot."

On January 3, 2014, Jared was admitted to Episcopal hospital, six-tenths of a mile from Brooke's house. He was diagnosed with pancreatitis, an inflammation of the pancreas most often caused by alcohol abuse. The pancreas is a small organ that sits behind the stomach, hidden inside the rib cage. It is essential to the digestion of food. Pancreatitis is said to feel like a burning knife twisted into your back. It can kill you.

On January 6, instead of accepting treatment for the pancreatitis, Jared discharged himself, AMA.

ooooo

Six months had passed since Maggie left Jared in an Alexandria hospital and went home to Mount Airy. She found a job tending bar. She knew Jared was still on the road, traveling with Aggro and Jimbo. She wanted to be out there with him. They kept in touch and tried to find a time and place to meet.

Jared's cell phone didn't save his sent texts, but it did keep Maggie's written to him:

> I want to see you too. I gotta make some money and get boots and a harness and stuff then Im out. So we can meet up somewhere soon if you want.

> Cause I'm just sad all the time here. I never sleep upstairs cause it makes me sad.

And Im gonna feel like shit for leaving mom but life is supposed to be happy and Im way better at being a shit talking drunk sign flying asshole than a biscuit.

Just housey problems I cant handle this. I'm misserable, it wasn't so bad when you were with me but it sucks. I love mom I just am not made to work and pay bills.

And yer the only person that understands or that I can talk to.

Send me a pic of u so I can smile.

There was one piece of dialogue on Maggie's phone. It began at 11:01 p.m. on January 10, 2014.

Maggie: Hope yer feeling good . . .

        Jared: Im kinda not okay. Im goin back to the hospit. I already tried once at the er today but the wait was too long.

Maggie: Oh no! What's wrong, how are you feeling now?

        Jared: I have pancriantidice. I don't know to spell it but it hurts like shit. I cant eat or drink and it hurts to walk. Plus iv been dtin all day cuz I cant drink my booze.

Maggie: I'd find something for pain to help you sleep till morning at least.

        Jared: Ya. Home girl down the street is goin to try and hook it up with some perc 10 or some zannys. Brook had been tryin to get her friend but she didn't pic up. Oh well. Ima just go back tomorrow morning.

Maggie: I'm glad you gots good people around you and I hope they have yer back like a butt crack!!! Oh

dude, gobs be careful and please
get better you can't leave yet, I
don't wanna follow into the dark
yet.

ooooo

No one knows when the last chance will come. But now we know that Jared had passed on more chances at staying out of the dark than made sense for a young man so sick. Now we know he was admitted to the Episcopal hospital a second time on Saturday, January 11, 2014. And we know that on January 13 he was in bed at the hospital when his mother called. She remembered what they said that day.

She said, "Jared, you gotta quit drinking or you'll die."

He said, "Mom, I don't want to die."

That Monday morning, a social worker named Deborah Lamb came to him with one more chance.

Episcopal called on Lamb to consult on patients with substance abuse issues. A week earlier, she had met Jared for the first time. "He was low-key, very polite, cordial," she told me two months after that meeting. "He wasn't rude or short with me. But he didn't spill his guts to me either." She remembered him because he was so young ("I usually get fifty- and sixty-year-olds") and because his visiting friends were unusual ("an artsy crowd, a lot of tattoos"). She said he had not been interested in talking about detoxification and rehabilitation.

The hospital administrators knew of Lamb's previous visit, so when the same young man with chronic alcoholism showed up again, they asked her to see him a second time. At Jared's bedside, she made her pitch again. She believes that at some time, maybe not now, maybe years from now, maybe when the patient has heard the pitch a hundred times, maybe then, he will hear it one more time and say yes. "The weight of it," Lamb said, "may finally be decisive."

Because she so often heard from alcoholics that they had no insurance and no money to pay for rehabilitation, Lamb came to Jared with an extraordinary offer. "I told him I could get him into detox and ninety-day rehab at a substance abuse facility for free."

She could do that through a Philadelphia County program called the Behavioral Health Special Initiative. He could get sober and he could get well. He could have a life that he chose rather than one chosen for him by bottom-shelf vodka. No one in any health system had ever made such a proposal to Jared. In response, Jared said what he had said so many times before.

"He sounded the same as the first time we talked," Lamb said. "He minimized his drinking. He said he'd 'cut down' because of the pain, 'cut down' from vodka to beer. They think that's the answer. But it's still alcohol. It's still the most deadly drug. And then they drink more beer—more alcohol—to get the same buzz they got from vodka."

As he had said no to Jeff and Lisa eighteen months earlier when they had gained him admission to the Boxwood substance abuse facility in Virginia, Jared now said no to Deborah Lamb in Philadelphia.

"How could he turn that down?" I asked Lamb.

She said, "The mistake we make with addicts is thinking they have any kind of logic."

There is a logic to it, only it's a logic of despair. Jay Davidson, the Louisville Healing Place administrator, said, "Jared said no for two reasons. One is that going through the withdrawal is physically, mentally, psychologically, and spiritually painful. The other part is the outright fear of living without the chemical, not being able to cope with life without it. We alcoholics have these feelings of guilt, shame, and remorse, feelings of 'I wish I could have, I should have, would have, but didn't.' So it's all those feelings of guilt and shame, and we can't deal with those feelings. It's emotional despair. So we drink for one reason: to change the way we feel."

It was 3:12 p.m. that day when Jared signed himself out of the hospital, AMA.

An hour later, he called me. All I knew then—I knew nothing of Deborah Lamb—was that he had been in Episcopal twice.

"How're you feeling now?" I asked.

"Just got out of the hospital," Jared said. "Feeling pretty good, actually. They gave me some Ativan, some morphine too, I think. Not in so much pain right now."

He said he needed money to buy three prescriptions. I thought the money might go for prescriptions, but I guessed it would buy vodka. I didn't know and I didn't care. If sending the money made me an enabler, so be it. I didn't ask a question, and if that makes me a poor grandfather and a worse reporter, so be it. All I cared about that day was helping my grandson the way he needed help.

"I'll get you the money, Western Union, right now," I said. "But, Jared, you know you gotta quit this."

"I know," he said.

"Take care. Love you, boy."

"Love you too," he said. "Tell Grandma hey and I love her."

At 4:45 p.m., I did a Western Union transfer of $100.

For the second time in seven days, Jared had said no to his best chance at finding a way out of the dark.

He returned to Kensington.

ooooo

Lynn had told him she would get the call. She told him she just knew it. Even the day before, she had warned him the drinking would kill him. She had tried to scare him straight by insisting on an answer to her question, "Cremation or burial?" She had said all that and still she was his mother and she really never thought the call would come. Something good would happen. He would find the right girl, there would be grandbabies and Christmas mornings and birthday parties. Someday they could remember the travelin' kids and the good times on trains and how harrowing it had been and how wonderful to have come through the dark into the light.

Jared left the Episcopal hospital on a pleasant winter day, mostly cloudy, fifty-two degrees, with a wind from the south-southeast at 9.2 miles per hour. There had been nine inches of snow in the new year, but none remained on the ground that day. Night had fallen by the time Jared returned to Brooke's row house.

Then, at 12:21 a.m. in Myrtle Beach on January 15, 2014, the call came.

The Philadelphia County medical examiner asked if he had reached the next of kin of Jared Kindred.

What he said next, the mother remembered only for the emptiness of the words, words she never wanted to hear, that could not be meant for her, and yet the man said the terrible words about her child, and months later she read the medical examiner's report and saw his words, whatever they had been, rendered clinically in a section called "Circumstances":

> Medics responded to a call for a person found down at his residence. They responded and found the decedent in agonal respirations. He was transported to the ER with oxygen. Upon arrival he was in asystole. He was intubated, given four rounds of epinephrine, one of bicarb, and one of calcium. All

attempts to revive him were unsuccessful and the decedent was pronounced.

The time of death was 1:45 a.m. January 14. Because the hospital could not immediately find a record of next of kin, it was nearly a full day later before the medical examiner called Lynn.

His report quoted Lynn:

"We just talked to him the day before. He had just gotten out of the hospital. He said he was doing fine. What the hell happened?"

Jacob heard the conversation and cried out, "No, no, *no*." It couldn't be Jared. He told his mother it had to be a mistake. Ask them, Mom. Ask them if they're sure. Ask about the tattoo.

Lynn said into the phone, "Can you tell me, is there a tattoo on his face?"

The man went away for a minute. On return he described the tattoo, and the medical examiner's report ended:

Mother of decedent was unable to continue conversation.

ooooo

Cheryl was watching television when she answered the phone at our home in Carlock, Illinois. She came to the foot of our bed. In the dark, she said six words.

"Jeff's on the phone."

I raised my head.

"Jared died."

It was 12:31 a.m. I dropped my head on the pillow. My greatest fear had been that I would hear those words. *Jared died*. Those words did not belong together. I felt time stop and start up, a heart-beat later. In that lost moment, those words emptied the bedroom of all but its darkness. I no longer felt the bed under me. I was suspended in a void, floating, feeling nothing. I got out of bed and embraced Cheryl. We wept and we wanted undone what was done.

TWENTY

The Scurvy Bastards came to the funeral. They came the way Jared would have wanted them to come. They came the way they lived. They came in dirty, stinking bib overalls held together by fraying twine and mismatched patches. The girls came with tangled dreads, the guys with beards gone wild.

At 1:09 p.m., Saturday, January 18, 2014, the funeral director said, "Thunder out there." He tilted his head toward the highway. I made a note of the time, the date, and the words. The reporter's work gave me a reason to look away from the casket. Grandfathers die, for they are old, and grandsons live on, for they will have children to raise and grandchildren to adore. A grandfather is out of place at his grandson's casket.

Jared's reddish beard had been trimmed to a perfect edge around his small, fine face. He wore brown Carhartt jeans, a white T-shirt, and, at his neck, a travelin' kid's bandanna, his "train rag" blackened by thousands of miles of road grime. A small boy had placed a Lego locomotive on Jared's chest. There, in the casket, he was Goblin, gone. There, in the casket, he was Jared, in my heart forever.

Jacob came up. One sidelong glance, he left.

Outside, Jacob stood with Jeff and they smoked cigarettes. Father and son said nothing.

Inside, a girl named Brandi came up to Jacob. Once a couple, they hadn't seen each other in a year.

"Why'd you come?" he asked.

"For my friend Jared," she said. "And to make sure you, the love of my life, are okay."

The thunder was the thrum of Harley-Davidsons. The local chapter of Hells Angels had asked its members to come to the funeral. Lynn and Joe Perron, her longtime boyfriend, were Harley people. These were not the Hells Angels raising hell at Altamont. These were middle-aged guys who were a threat only to sell you insurance.

A bright young girl came to the funeral. Samantha Street, sixteen years old, knew Jared as the cute guy she saw maybe once a year at his mother's house, two doors down in their Myrtle Beach neighborhood. In the chapel, Samantha asked her mother about those people in the dirty, stinking clothes.

"They're from Jared's world," the mother said. "They jump trains to different parts of the country."

"What about their home, their family?" the girl said. "And where is the rest of their stuff?"

"They don't have homes, honey. They are each other's family. And all they have is what they can put in their backpacks."

As much as they could, the Bastards had shined themselves up. They were quiet, respectful, dignified. They sat a row ahead of Samantha, and she saw tears and she saw tangled dreads leaning against beards gone wild. Later, for a high school English class, she wrote about the Scurvy people:

"When I first saw them, they stood huddled together, holding one another and offering kind words of support. They did not care about the bewildered looks some threw their way. All they cared about was being there for one another. I was in absolute awe. It tugged at my heart to see such loving people so deeply affected by the passing of a dear friend."

I looked for a girl I had never seen.

I wanted to meet Maggie.

I saw a girl who couldn't walk into the chapel.

She was tiny and pretty with the faintest of tattooed lines on her cheeks. She came to the chapel's wide doorway. She leaned forward to look around the corner, a little at a time, as if in fear of seeing what she knew she would see. The casket was thirty feet away. She stopped. She dropped her face into her hands, turned, and went to another room.

That girl sat on a couch, and I took a place next to her.

"Are you Maggie?" I said. "I'm Jared's grandfather."

She leaned her head against my shoulder.

"Thanks for being so good for Jared," I said, and she whispered, "The best time of my life."

From the chapel, I heard Arlo Guthrie singing about a train called the *City of New Orleans*, rolling on Illinois Central lines . . .

Jared's friends had asked for the song to be played under a slideshow of his life, the train of a travelin' kid's dreams singing good night, America . . .

Under the music, a slideshow . . . we saw Jared with Maggie twice, three times, four, five, eight times. The two of them golden in sunlight. Sleeping, his forehead on her shoulder. In rubble alongside railroad tracks, laughing, mugging for the camera, a twelve-pack of Busch in their happy hands . . . we saw again the picture of Jeff, the new father, twenty-six years old, with a week-old son in the crook of each arm, his face made soft and radiant by joy. "My country boys," he had called the twins, "Jake and Jed." And we saw again, wonderfully, Goblin and Booze Cop, shoulder to shoulder, lost under the grime and tattoos, looking at us and daring us to think of them as anything other than brothers.

We had come from Illinois. The Scurvy people had found their way from Maine and Florida, from Louisiana and North Carolina, from California and Indiana. Every picture in the slideshow was prettier than the last, and I loved those moments when Jared laughed for the camera. I knew those were moments of light in a life of darkness, and yet, I asked Aggro, "Was he always like that?"

"I don't know what it was about Goblin," she said. "But that kid could take a shit pile and turn it into gold. You want to talk about perfect? Goblin was everyone's sunshine."

"'Everywhere's sunshine'?" I said.

"Every*one's.*"

"I thought you said 'every*where's* sunshine.'"

"That too," Aggro said. "Goblin was *everywhere's* sunshine."

The funeral's preacher came properly dressed, in blue jeans and bike leathers. He was passionate about Jesus Christ and redemption and heaven. But he didn't know Jared, and he said nothing he couldn't have said of anyone in the room. When he finished, he asked if anyone wanted to speak.

Yes, I would speak. I remembered that day along a creek in a pasture when I refused to get in a picture of my dying father surrounded by his friends and family. In his dying days, I had not been able to tell Dad I loved him. And I had passed on a chance to kneel at his side in that picture and I had lived to regret it. I would speak this time. I would be with Jared one more time. I stood and looked around the room. I saw Lynn and Maggie and Booze Cop and Jeff and Jacob.

I said, "No offense to my wife, Cheryl, who is at my side here, but when we got married, I was twenty-one years old and I knew nothing. When we had our son, Jeff, I was twenty-two, and I knew nothing then either. But when Jared and Jacob were born, I was forty-seven, and I finally knew something. I knew that life was a miracle, and I knew those boys were proof that miracles happen."

Baptist preachers say they start talking and God takes over. They may be right. I had no idea I would say what I said next.

"Again, no offense to my wife and our son," I said, "but I know I never loved anyone more than I loved those boys. I loved Jared, and I love Jacob, to use the biblical phrase, with the love that surpasses all understanding."

On our trip to Myrtle Beach for the funeral, Cheryl said she didn't know if she could handle it. She wasn't sure she could see Jared without breaking down. Once there, she could not see him enough. Before she left his side the last time, her fingers trembling, she touched his beard, ever so lightly. And I kissed his forehead, ever so lightly.

When Lynn stood at her child's side and wept, Jacob went to her. "Mom, please don't cry," he said. "Jared was all about making people happy."

Then Jacob stood alone and talked to his brother. We could not hear him, but we saw the last words. He said, "I love you."

TWENTY-ONE

Everyone followed the Harleys' thunder from the funeral service to a wake at Donny's Saloon, a bikers' bar on the edge of Myrtle Beach. A hundred people crowded around the bar and lined up at a buffet table under television screens showing the day's sports events. Lynn raised a toast in her son's honor, asking everyone to share a thing he had created. She called out to the rowdy crowd, "Let's do a 'Jared shot'!"

A Jared shot came with broccoli, not alcohol. Conceived over dinner at his mother's, it was a sprig of cauliflower and a stalk of broccoli slathered with ranch dressing and served in a small plastic cup.

The small moment moved Jeff to Lynn's side. Divorced almost twenty years, they had shared custody, and both were involved in their sons' lives. There was never more than an uneasy truce between them until Jeff nibbled at his Jared shot and told Lynn, "I'm so sorry I was so mean to you for so many years. Let's be friends." As young marrieds, they had been motorcycle people. Now they embraced in a bikers' bar.

For the first time since October at Jeff's place, I saw Aggro. Everything she'd ever said about Jared and their life on the road I took as the best information available. We moved to a side of the room, away from the hubbub.

I said, "Aggro, I'm going to play the devil's advocate here. I need to know why Jared was in that life. You know as well as I do that people see you all as damaged goods. You're all from broken homes, you're running from pain and everyone who caused that pain—parents, preachers, police. What if I said the pain cast darkness over every day and you self-medicate with alcohol and other drugs. What if I called you lost, wasted souls?"

Aggro had heard that speech before. "I could talk for days," she said. "I'll just write you a letter pretty soon, after we're done with all this." Two weeks later came the letter. She wrote:

We're not lost, we're not suffering. We ride freight trains for the same reason a major league baseball player plays ball! For the love of the game! It is for the sheer joy of freedom and a love for life. Haven't you ever done something that was a little crazy, a little scary and amazing and superfun all at the same time—and then thought, "Man! I wish I could do that for the rest of my life." We were brave—reckless, dauntless, really—enough to do it! No holds barred, all chips in, ballsy enough to forsake all that Americans hold dear and plunge headfirst into the unknown. THAT'S what riding freight is all about. If we didn't want to do it, we wouldn't.

Your grandson was better than the kid in that movie, Into the Wild. *Goblin wasn't some pseudo-philosopher who didn't know shit about living. He didn't keep a journal or wax poetical. He wore his heart on his sleeve. He didn't have complexities. He was just like every other hobo! He found something he loved and ran with it. We play at the highest stakes in the WORLD! We are the rock stars of the streets. We scavenge, pillage, and ride off into the sunset. Land pirates! We are all flames burning brightly, and some of us are snuffed out, never getting a chance to burn down to an ember.*

Quit asking, "Why, why, why" about Goblin. I can't tell you, he couldn't tell you, and neither can any other 'bo. Just like the old cowboys and wanderers of yore, we all have our demons and skeletons in our closets, but we don't let them define us. Goblin was a great kid and an even better hobo. He could ride hard with the best of us. He wasn't running from anything! He ran into the arms of life, took it by the horns, and made it his bitch.

○○○○○

After promising me that letter, Aggro hugged me and said, "Now I'm going to find out what the hell happened to my little brother."

She walked over to a woman I didn't know. What they said, I couldn't hear. But the body language was clear. Aggro was in the woman's face. Every time the woman leaned away, Aggro leaned into her, squared up, shoulders back. After two or three minutes, the woman went out to the parking lot. Aggro followed her.

When Aggro returned, I asked, "What's going on?"

"Her story keeps changing."

"Who's 'her'?"

"Brooke. From Philly."

"What's she saying?"

"That she didn't know what happened that night," Aggro said.

"Looked like you weren't buying it."

"No way. Finally, in the parking lot, I got the story."

"And what is it?"

"You don't want to know," Aggro said.

"I'm a grown-up. I can handle it."

Aggro told me enough and I learned more.

Fifteen minutes after I sent the Western Union $100 to him, Jared picked up the money. It was dark on the barren moonscape of Kensington when he returned to Brooke's discolored row house with its iron-barred windows. Because it was what they did when there was nothing else to do, the five people in the house, including Jared, began drinking. For three days in the Episcopal hospital, doctors had sent morphine, Ativan, and Dilaudid into Jared's bloodstream. At Brooke's, he added alcohol's poison.

Brooke was in the house along with a couple other people, including one of Jared's longtime road friends, Pixie. They all were broke—except for Jared, who had my $100. Because he came to the house suffering the unrelenting pain of pancreatitis, someone suggested heroin. Pixie had never seen Jared do any drugs other than alcohol, but on that night the travelers needed/wanted more than booze. Pixie later told friends, "Then everyone fell out. We got sold messed-up bags."

It was after midnight when Pixie saw Brooke and Jared unconscious in the living room. "Someone called 911," Pixie later said, "but it was already too late for Goblin. We couldn't bring him back."

When I talked with Brooke, she denied suggesting the dope. "Everyone's wanting to blame somebody, and I'm the one they're blaming. But it's just not true. I hadn't done dope since I was nineteen, and I'm thirty-three now and I wanted it? That's crazy. I'd told everyone no dope in my house. . . . I can't blame anyone. Jared was a good guy, but he was also an adult and could make his own decisions. If he wanted to take dope, no one forced him. He had been talking about it for a while only because he was in so much pain, he couldn't take the pain anymore."

Twelve days after Jared's death, upset by the confrontation with Aggro at the wake in Myrtle Beach, Brooke sent a text to Lynn. It read, in part:

> I'm sorry you are going through so much pain. But I need a break. I came all the way down to the funeral to pay respect to my boyfriend who I loved dearly. But I got yelled at by 12 people I don't even know, blaming me and saying I was lying. Yes, that night was blurry for everyone. But I took care of Jared. I did everything I could to make him safe. I brought him into my home, fed him, and did everything I could to ensure his well-being. I loved him and I wouldn't do that for just anyone. I was with him at the hospital every day with my friends, not his friends, trying to get him to go to detox/rehab. I dropped a lot of my life because I cared about him so much so. So if those people can't see that, they are just a piece of shit. I'm sorry, but *none* of them were there for him.

Neither Maggie nor Aggro was in Philadelphia that night. They believed Jared had fallen in with people who didn't know how to help him. "Somebody had to have persuaded Jared to do dope," Maggie said. "If you lined up big piles of every drug on a table, cocaine, weed, meth, heroin, crack, molly, and said, 'Take your pick,' Jared would have said, 'Naw, gimme my vodka.'" Aggro said, "It wouldn't have happened if I was there. I'd have said, 'Here's eight ibuprofen, take 'em.'"

Jared's death was first attributed to "chronic alcoholism." Toxicology reports later cited "drug intoxication." Lynn knew that Jared's body likely had reached its limits of recovery from pancreatitis. She asked the Philadelphia pathologist the only question that mattered to her. She told him her son had been in pain for years. In his final moments, was he in agony?

The pathologist, Aaron Rosen, said no. When Jared lost consciousness that night, he would have been in no pain. He would have felt good.

"So my child went to sleep," Lynn said, knowing it to be true and finding in that truth a kind of peace, "and he will never be hurt again."

TWENTY-TWO

I went to Mount Airy the month after Jared's funeral. I sat with Maggie in her mother's little living room, three or four steps from the stairway to the attic bedroom she had shared with Jared. We talked for three hours. She was bright and sober and focused, and we talked about dogs and cats and many things. We left the house to see Mount Airy. We drove past the Red Barn and past the Earle. We had a hamburger at Barney's Cafe, and we coaxed a tourist to take a photo of us by the Andy and Opie statue. How I wish it had worked for Maggie and Jared, for Maggie, tiny, gorgeous Maggie, had known Jared at his best and his worst, and she wanted to be with him always.

Of course I loved Maggie, why wouldn't I? Jared had loved her. But after 2014, I lost track of her as I struggled in the reporting and writing of this book. In December 2015, my wife suffered a major stroke and I wrote nothing for almost two years. On getting back to work, my first order of business was to find Maggie. In the winter of 2016, she did a Facebook post of Dixie curled up on a bed, with the caption: "Dixie Dog is back in Texas and loving the home sweet home I made for us. Hard work pays off." She was in Austin.

She had passed through the city in her train-hopping years and always liked it. Now she had a job—$12 an hour washing dishes at a Tex-Mex restaurant. She also had an apartment and a car. It was close to the real-world living that she and Jared once had thought might be theirs. By the time we met up in the fall of 2017, Maggie had been in Austin a year. It was, she said, "the longest I have stayed anywhere in more than nine years."

Maggie was twenty-seven years old. The day we talked in Walnut Creek Park, she looked strong and healthy, though much thinner than when I'd seen her last. She had outlived maybe two dozen of her road dogs, and now she thought she might outlive the Maggie she had been, the Maggie who grew up in New York City partying her ass off, the Maggie who had grown accustomed to thinking of vodka by the half-gallons as all in a day's fun.

She said she was sober for the first time since she left Mount Airy as a teenage parolee from a detention center. She was using no alcohol, no other drugs, and had been admitted to a city drug rehab program. Even the thought of drinking, she said, now made her sick to her stomach: "I can't tell you the last time I had a drink." More important, she said, "I've dropped my I-don't-give-a-fuck attitude."

She now cared about things that once didn't matter. Her mother, for one. They had reconnected in Jared's time, first through Maggie's drive from Houston to North Carolina with Jared almost certainly dying in the car's back seat. Now, on her own in Austin, Maggie discovered that she was not alone after all; her mother bought her the car and helped with rent. After ten years and more of not giving a fuck whether the sun came up in the morning, Maggie now made each day a challenge. She told me, "I'm writing. You wouldn't believe it, but I am. I want to write and make money at it."

What I'd read of her stuff told me she had a distinctive way with language and a feel for the rhythm of a story. But the distance is great from ambition to reality. Could she ever be a writer? I knew the answer to that question would be found in the answer to another: Could she defeat addiction?

On December 8, 2017, on what would have been Jared's twenty-ninth birthday, Maggie did a Facebook post:

"Yer my sugarplum, pumpdee dee ummp dee umppp kin, yer my sweetie pie . . . and I want you to know that I love you so and ill always be right heeere . . . that's why I sing these songs to you . . . because you are sooooo dear!!!" All the nights you sung that song to me, more than I can count. And on the nights I feel like I wont make it or even just cant sleep I replay those memories, on nights that are going along just fine I sing it then too . . . along with a thousand other memories. I'm still close behind. Happy barrrfffday my goblin king. I miss you rotttssss and rotsss and I love you rottts and rottts. Gobledegook. Boop boop. "Ridiculous nation station. Can you imagine imagining" Not a day goes by. A year ago, remember, I was on a badass high wall grainer riding through Virginia on yer birthday and you were in my pocket—your ashes that Mama Tiger gave me—with vodka in my other hand. And for the first time in a long time I felt content. I miss you so much my love. My promise is still up, the world is still ridiculous nation station, and I still miss you. I know your watching over all of us and keeping us well and safe, I love you, happy birthday sea turtle!!!!

She said goodbye with haunting words.

See you soon.

TWENTY-THREE

On a spring morning in 2014, I met Aggro near the central fountain in Chicago's Grant Park. Our meeting followed closely on the arrest of three train-hoppers for a murder in California.

Reports of that killing had moved on the road dogs' grapevine to Jared and Maggie in Mount Airy. The victim was a nineteen-year-old college student. John Alpert had told his family he was going to the Roseville train yard to try a great adventure, train-hopping. His family last heard from him on March 13, 2013. Two months later, his body was discovered by a creek near a Roseville hop-out spot. The cause of death was blunt force trauma.

Aggro told me she knew the three people arrested. She said a detective had called her. In his investigation he had come across her phone number. That was all he wanted, she said, nothing more, a routine call. I had no reason to think otherwise.

Aggro was in Chicago only for the day. She wanted to find a railroad yard where she could catch out to Minneapolis. We drove from Grant Park out to Blue Island and around to Bensenville. Finally, giving up on a freight, I delivered her to a bus station downtown.

"Be safe," I said.

"I'm glad you didn't say 'goodbye,'" she said. "Saying 'goodbye' is like saying you'll never see that person again. Out here, that happens all the time." She remembered Jared's reaction when he saw a friend, Tim Slade, for the first time in months. "He was just so excited. That's how he always was with seeing people he knew. No matter if they were his best friends or just acquaintances, he was always happy to see people still alive."

He was always happy to see people still alive. Said so matter-of-factly she might have been saying he was happy to see people wearing shoes. Death was a fact of life out there. Michael Stephen guessed that Jared, in five years, had called to report the deaths of thirty travelin' kids. As we walked to the bus station, Aggro said her only worry about dying was who would take care of her dog, Tobias. "He'd just be curled up against my dead body," she said.

She hefted a mammoth backpack onto her thick shoulders and walked in the night's rain to Union Station. She would catch a Megabus to Minneapolis. At her side, Tobias.

Less than three months later, on July 1, I saw a news story out of Roseville, California.

4TH SUSPECT ARRESTED IN TRAIN-HOPPING MURDER

A fourth suspect in the beating death of 19-year-old John Paul Alpert was arrested Sunday in Washington, just days after Roseville police announced a warrant for the suspect's arrest. According to Roseville Police Spokeswoman Dee Dee Gunther, 28-year-old Charity Ann Williams was arrested Sunday. . . .

Earlier this year, Laura Kenner, Edward Anauo, and Jules Carrillo were arrested and charged with Alpert's murder. As detectives continued to investigate the case, they recently obtained probable cause to arrest Williams.

I spoke with a Roseville reporter, Scott Thomas Anderson, as he worked on a story about the woman I knew as Aggro.

"She was smart, articulate, insightful, self-confident, and unafraid," I told him. "I'm stunned and saddened."

The reporter said he knew no details about Aggro's alleged involvement in the murder. He suggested, probably from conversations with the local police, that the beating happened because the neophyte Alpert committed some "breach of etiquette" that angered the veteran train-hoppers. They then left him unconscious. Under California law, that would be first-degree murder based on "callous disregard for life."

Early in 2018, after the other three defendants pleaded guilty and after insisting she wanted to go to trial, Aggro finally pleaded guilty. She was sentenced to fifteen to thirty years in prison.

TWENTY-FOUR

On May 12, 2014, Cheryl and I made our second trip to Myrtle Beach. We returned for Jacob's graduation from the Pittsburgh Institute of Aeronautics. He wore a dark suit, gray shirt, and blue tie. He had waxed his mustache and carefully fashioned its tips into curlicues. He was by God beautiful.

He sat with ten other graduates on a dais before a small crowd of family and friends at the PIA offices. In the aviation mechanics classrooms, he had earned all As and Bs. He had passed exams on airframe and power plant mechanics. That morning he had done the final orals to become a Federal Aviation Administration–certified mechanic. He was proud of his achievement and particularly proud to have persevered.

"There was one semester I had to skip, and Mom told me that most people, when they lay out a semester in college, they never go back," he said. "So I said, 'No way, fuck that. I'm going back, I'm finishing.' Then, the last semester, which began two days after

Jared died, it was hard. It wasn't the challenge intellectually. It was keeping my mind off things."

Never a good student, Jacob had attended his high school graduation reluctantly, just glad to be done. He had dropped out of a local community college after one semester. Until the two years at PIA, he was no less a wanderer through life than Jared had been.

"Even sitting up there, waiting during the ceremony," Jacob said, "I thought, *They're not going to call my name.* Weird, I knew I had graduated. But it was still a lot of being nervous. It didn't seem real. It wasn't that I thought it would never happen. At the start, maybe, I didn't think I could actually do it. And then I did it. I was walking up to get my FAA certificate."

Once, Jared had kept track of Jacob's progress in school and joked about Jacob's "big-ass house" with a room in it for him. On graduation day, with his FAA certificate on his bedside table, Jacob told me that story again. I had come to his room at his mother's house to say to him what I had never been smart enough to say to his brother.

I had known only the broadest outlines of what addiction meant. Of how it happened, what it did to a person's brain, I knew nothing. Now I knew more than I ever wanted to know. I could not come to Jacob's graduation—his entry into a life with direction— without telling him what I had learned in moving from naivete to an understanding of addiction. No need to tell Jacob that his brother was an alcoholic; he knew that. But I needed to have this conversation. I had failed to say the cold, hard truth to Jared when it might have made a difference. Damned if I would fail to say it to Jacob.

"Jared was an alcoholic," I said. "He was addicted to alcohol. Do you know, Jacob, how addiction works?"

He sat silent.

"You drink vodka, your brain makes you feel good. You keep drinking, you need more and more to get the same feel-good. Pretty soon, and I say this hoping I scare the shit out of you, you drink enough and you're dead."

Jacob made an odd analogy. "Yeah, like when you use too much Chapstick. The body produces moisture naturally. But if you use Chapstick all the time, the body stops producing it and you have to use it all the time. Like that."

"Except using Chapstick doesn't kill you," I said.

We sat in his bedroom at his mother's house. To be certain I said everything I wanted to say, I had made notes on a legal pad. I left the page with Jacob:

1. Addiction is a family disease.
2. You are at risk.
3. The disease came to own Jared.
4. It literally rewires your brain.
5. For an alcoholic/addict, logical thinking can become impossible.
6. The addict thinks of the substance as a nutrient. He not only wants it, he demands it, he needs it.
7. You must know the signs of addiction in order to ask for help.
8. Ask for help. It's there.
9. But know this. You must ask the instant you suspect addiction. If Jared could have asked for help, he would have.
10. David Sheff: "Addiction is not a character flaw, not a moral failing. It's an illness and it can be treated. Ask for help."

"Jared said the right thing when he told your mother he'd wash away booze," I said. "But he was no longer in control. The substance was. The vodka was. The addiction was. He once owned the substance, but then the substance owned him."

I talked about my father's own killing addiction—to cigarettes. "From the time he was twelve, my Dad smoked. All through his life, World War II, after, he smoked until he got lung cancer and died. He was only fifty-one, Jacob, fifty-one—and I'm twenty years older than that now. I never smoked, maybe because our sports coaches told us not to. But I never once thought of smoking after Dad died. I was scared of smoking." And I said, "Jacob, be scared of drinking."

That day he drove us to the airport for our flight home. He hugged me, kissed Cheryl on the cheek, and said, "I'm so happy you came."

"Be safe, take care of yourself, come to Illinois and stay with us anytime," I said.

As he drove away, Jacob waved and called out, "Love you both."

He was gone before I whispered, "Love you, boy." I whispered not to Cheryl and not to myself. I whispered the words to both boys that I once held in the palms of my hands.

TWENTY-FIVE

Nine months after Jared's death, Lynn and I went to New Orleans for Halloween. It was his favorite city and his favorite time. The idea was to walk where he had walked and see what he had seen. She brought along a vial of his ashes to be spread on the wooden steps of a wharf at the Mississippi's edge. They were ancient steps where the Scurvy Bastards had been conceived. Lynn believed that if we were there, on those steps, in New Orleans, on Halloween, Jared would be there with us.

We stopped and sat on the sidewalk outside the Bubba Gump Shrimp Company restaurant at 429 Decatur Street. We sat with Lyndzy and another of Jared's pals, Shamus, until a policeman, at 10:03 p.m., saw the four of us and said, "You two know better," meaning Lyndzy and Shamus knew better than to sit on the sidewalk, which can get a travelin' kid a ticket in NOLA, and they should move along and take the old folks with them.

"Where to now?" Shamus asked us.

"The steps," Lynn said.

We walked north. Everywhere along the street, Jared was there.

We stopped at a red door alongside the Big Easy Daiquiris and pizza shop, the door described by Christine Maynard in her piece about Sarafina Scarlet, the singer with a baseline of grit who sat on the stoop with her guitar. The door opens to a passage leading to 907A, Christine's old apartment, where Jared had slept on her Italian leather couch, where they had gone to the roof to see parades and sunsets. I wanted to go in. But the door was locked. A mailbox was stuffed with envelopes postmarked months earlier.

We passed a cream-colored building, the Jax Brewery where Jared and Puzzles danced on the rooftop, where Jared slept on gravel alongside railroad tracks at the back of the building. Past Jackson Square, where Jared arranged Sarafina's marriage to Patrizio, and we walked through the Café du Monde, where Jared and Stray Falldowngoboom scooped up beignets left by tourists. We stopped at a fountain to talk with Dice. He had lost an arm and leg rescuing his dog from under a moving train. He knew Jared as Goblin. "Beautiful kid," Dice said. "He introduced me to my girlfriend, Fluff." Booze Cop was next to Dice. "This fountain," Booze Cop said, sitting on its edge, "Goblin and me used to scoop out change to buy the next drink."

We met a bulky guy named Dragon. Dragon, who said he was thirty-four years old and had done two tours of Army duty in Iraq and Afghanistan. Dragon, melancholy on this night: "Losing too many friends. Couple dozen this year. If it's not OD'ing, it's booze. If it's not booze, a train. If not a train, cops." He asked what Lynn and I were doing in New Orleans. "Just wanting to do what Jared did," I said, and Dragon asked, "You smoke weed? Goblin woulda made Bob Marley proud."

Dragon led us to the wharf. Its steps were massive, with treads three feet wide and thirty feet from end to end. They were wide, thick wooden beams embedded in a levee descending to the river. How massive the trees must have been that gave up those steps. Steps made to last forever.

"Here's where Jared was," Lynn said. She sat on the right side of the steps near a waist-high piling. A thick rope was threaded through that piling to the next one down. Lynn had seen a photograph of travelin' kids on the steps. She had seen her child on that spot. She said, "Here's where we'll do the ashes tomorrow."

Walking back along Decatur Street that night, we watched two police officers dealing with six home bums in various stages of drunkenness, some passed out, everyone wasted, all gathered in a tiny green space around a statue of Jean-Baptiste Le Moyne de Bienville, an early governor of Louisiana and the founder of New Orleans in 1718.

"You guys want to have a better time in New Orleans?" one cop said to the bums. "Stop getting fucked up! I don't want to bother you, but get up, put your pants on, take a walk right now."

He was ten minutes into writing tickets when I asked, "What do you cite them for?"

"It's called 'disturbing the peace by tumultuous behavior,'" he said.

"But you don't arrest them?"

"God, no," the cop said. "If we arrest them drunk or on drugs, we have to take them to the hospital. And the nurses have more power than God. We'd have to stay there while they run medical exams, and we'd have to do paperwork out our asses. We'd be there all night."

The other cop, older than his patrol partner, asked Lynn and me, "What are y'all doing here?"

Lynn explained.

"Let me ask another question," the cop said. "You don't have to answer. You look like good people. But your son, your grandson, what happened that he was out here?"

Of course he asked that question. Everyone asks how he came to live out there. At breakfast the day of Jared's funeral, Mark, a friend of forty years, had asked Jeff that question. "No idea," Jeff said, "none at all." To the cop in New Orleans, Lynn said, "I don't know." And the cop nodded, for if anyone knows that life is a riddle never solved, a cop walking mean streets at midnight knows it.

Back in our hotel, Lynn and I talked into the morning hours. It had been a boy's lifetime and more since she stood at my desk in Georgia and asked if it would be okay to marry my son. That day I asked her for twins tomorrow. She gave them to me. I loved her for that then and loved her for it now, in New Orleans, along the Mississippi River and on Decatur Street and in Jackson Square, all the places where we felt Jared's presence.

At last she had enjoyed a day when everything and everyone reminded her of her child.

She said, "It was so great to come here. I feel so much better. Now I know he had fun here."

"And how do you know that?" I said.

She laughed. "Because I'm having fun here."

On a bright Halloween afternoon, we returned to the steps along the Mississippi. Lyndzy was there with Booze Cop, Tammy, Shamus, Dragon, and maybe two dozen other travelin' kids. Some came with guitars, one with a washboard and spoons, everyone filthy and stinking and happy to be where they fit. And at 4:57 p.m., Lyndzy shouted to the crowd on the steps, "Everybody, we're here to honor Goblin. We're here with his mama, Mama Tiger, and who else's mama would come here to be with us? We're gonna spread some of Goblin's ashes here on the steps and . . ."

Not everyone noticed Lyndzy talking. Not everyone fell into a respectful silence in memory of Goblin. Maybe they just didn't know how to act on a solemn occasion. So Dragon instructed them, "*Shut the fuck up!*"

Then Lyndzy poured Jared's ashes from a vial onto the step where he once sat. As a breeze caught the falling, floating stream of ashes and spread them away from the spot on the wharf step, someone said, "Pour beer on 'em to keep 'em there," and someone else said, "No, Goblin would hate that, wasting beer," and laughter fell on the boy's ashes, and I believe Jared was there, laughing.

EPILOGUE

I miss Jared. The phone rings, I want it to be him.
Now I know some of what happened and enough of the why.
I learned the geography of his life on the road and the ferocity of
his addiction. Did I, in telling his story, cut Jared some slack? Absolutely. I believed what Ash Dogskin believed. The Lakota Sioux
called Jared "my *heyoka*," the tribe's sacred clown empowered to
heal wounds, psychic and physical. When the soundtrack of Jared's
life was the nihilistic roaring of freight trains, I also heard songs
of redemption. They sang of a joyful animation and goofy po-
etry that distinguished Goblin from the crowd. *Everywhere's sunshine . . . Naked girls, Grandpa, and they're running through the forest,
naked . . . The cute little flirt . . . The happiest guy I'd ever seen . . .*

A grandfather knows a grandson's life moves away from his.
But I had never imagined Jared gone, let alone gone to a place
where every question brought back dark answers. Until too late, I
did not recognize his pain; by the time I understood an alcoholic's
despair, I could not help him. But I so loved the boy that I could

not let stand the idea that I had lost him forever. To know what happened, to know the answers, even the darkest of them, was to hold him near again.

All these months becoming years, I have looked at passing trains. At a crossing gate, I told Cheryl, "See that car with the V-shapes? It's a grainer. On each end, that's the porch. Jared rode there." The train shook the ground under us. Cheryl said, "My God."

I went to the local hardware store for nails. One aisle over, Carhartt overalls.

In Augusta, Georgia, on my way to the Masters, I drove past a couple dozen CSX freight cars sided out. CSX, Jared's favorite line.

Our Walmart has a bank where I did Western Union money transfers to Jared. Even a year later, the man behind the counter, expecting to make another transaction, made eye contact with me.

The coroner's office in Philadelphia returned Jared's belongings to his mother. The package included his backpack. The backpack included his Carhartt bib overalls. In a pocket of the bibs, the hugs-and-kisses seashell.

ooooo

Off the road, trying to be sober, Booze Cop found a job.

Stray operated rides at a traveling carnival. She got married.

The girl named Bird sent a note: "When I found out Goblin was gone, I cried in the street like a little girl and I didn't care who fucking saw. That year, 2014, I rode hard a lot and finally got some work in California and I miss riding right now. So many things I wish I could tell my friend. He would be so happy that I'm doing so good. Haven't seen CSX in a while, which is really weird for me. I hope next time I'm on a freight that when that metal melody starts to sing me to sleep, I hope he's riding with me. I miss you, Goblin."

Aggro wrote long letters from jail. In the spring of 2018, my friend Patti Parker and I visited Aggro in a California prison. We sat at one of two dozen tables in a sunny visitors' room. Patti had known only the road dog Aggro of my stories, a young woman she'd seen photographed in an orange jailhouse jumpsuit, her dark hair buzzed into a bizarre cut. Now Patti saw Charity Ann Williams, healthy and vibrant, and called her "beautiful with long, wavy blonde hair." A tattoo on her cheek carried Jared's initials and, in the ink, ashes from his cremation. As part of the rehabilitation process, Aggro was required to tell of her crime; so we heard how it happened and how she used a frying pan and her dog's food dish to dig a burial spot for young John Alpert along a creek. "I've been baptized in here," Aggro said, "and I've prayed for John's parents." At age thirty-two, she is in for fifteen to thirty years, with a first parole hearing on February 2, 2027. I asked how much of our conversation I could use in this book. "All of it," she said. "Tell the whole story, nothing but the story. It's important for your readers to know what this kind of behavior can lead to—without villainizing the community." Before we left, we heard in the near-distance a train's lonesome whistle blowing. Aggro turned her head toward the sound and said, "It put me here, but I love it." Her voice went soft. "Now I hear it and can't get to it."

In Myrtle Beach, a kitten cried. Lynn had heard the sound in the night and discounted it; morning came, she walked outside. There the kitten cowered against her garage, a tiny thing, a muted calico, gray with orange splotches. Lynn believed fate had delivered the kitten. On the same date, August 3, five years earlier, Jared had allowed Craig AntiHero to do the facial tattoo. Also, Lynn noticed that the kitten had a broken tail. "Like my broken heart," she said. She had three cats, Sunday, Havana, and Corona—spoiled pets of the sort that had caused Jared to say he would like, someday, to come back as one of his mother's cats. Now she had four cats because the calico, once in her house, curled up atop a couch, "like she belonged there." Lynn named the kitten Goblin.

Lyndzy, Jared's first romance on the road, married Jimbo, who had been with Jared the day we saw them in Orange. Lyndzy and Jimbo became parents. They named their daughter Kindred.

ooooo

Friends have assumed that doing this book must have been cathartic. No. Across five years, the reporting and writing were the most painful I have ever done. I am haunted by the eviscerating horrors of alcoholism. And our family, like many, has wounds it wants to forget, but a telling of Jared's story would not allow me that privilege. No, no catharsis. The work extended the sadness by telling me more than any grandfather wants to know about either his grandson or himself.

Cheryl and I sat with the preacher who had done my mother's funeral. His name was Maurice Stribling. "Call me Skeet, everyone does," he said. Skeet had the look of an Old Testament prophet, a wizened face encircled by a snowy white beard. In the way lives intersect in a small Illinois town, he was the pastor at the Atlanta Christian Church where, a lifetime earlier, I had attended Sunday school so I could sit with my third-grade girlfriend, Luanne.

"Christians believe God has compassion on all that he has made," Skeet said. "I take comfort in that because we don't know what personal demons people have been fighting. I trust in a compassionate God to see truly into our hearts. We are not in a position, as God is, to measure what value a life has produced. It's not the years that determine our value. You can live to be a hundred and not contribute to others. Then again, you could die at twenty after contributing tremendously. Your grandson shared love and brought love into your life. Even his struggles contributed to your life. Even his final loss contributed to your life. What he gave you and Cheryl, in his short time, helped make your lives what they are."

On January 14, 2019, five years after Jared's death, I sat with Cheryl in the nursing home where my mother had died and where Cheryl, after her stroke in December of 2015, became a resident; she is an invalid who cannot communicate. I showed her the portrait of Jared and Jacob, three years old, the world champion twins, golden in their white tuxedoes. She looked at the picture for five, six, seven seconds. I wondered what she saw, if anything, and wondered what she remembered, if anything. Then came an answer. She smiled a soft, sweet grandmother's smile.

I remembered a day in July 1997. Jared was eight years old. We had gone exploring, a grandpa and a boy. He rode behind me on an ATV. We bounced around our Virginia farmland. We rode up and down hills, through great stands of trees, along a waterfall that fed Russell Run, which ran to the Rappahannock River, which ran to the Chesapeake Bay, which became the Atlantic Ocean. We rode for an hour or so and then, late in the afternoon, we stopped on a rise in a pasture.

I said, "Look at the sky, Jared, it's pretty."

The day's fading sun had dropped near the horizon behind a cottony blanket of clouds.

Jared said, "See those?" He pointed to puffs of clouds. "Those are angels looking over us."

I saw the angels and I saw the sun soft on them and I saw shimmering rays of gold streaming through the clouds into the sky. Jared saw more.

He said, "That looks like the gateway to heaven."

ACKNOWLEDGMENTS

I could not and would not have written this book without Lynn Ann Sigda's blessing and trust. Nor would I have done it if Jared's twin, Jacob, had gone silent. Instead, like his mother, Jacob asked me to tell Jared's story in full and tell it truly. My son, Jeff, and his wife, Lisa, answered every question, however uncomfortable the question, however painful the answer. I pray that all of them— mother, brother, father, stepmother—find peace in confirmation of what they believed. Jared was loved by everyone who knew him.

I can testify to that love because my reporting put me in Jared's world on the road. There I met his friends. By then he was alive only in their memories. Yet they spoke of him so vividly, as the essence of happiness, that a grandfather could be forgiven for thinking the boy might at any minute dance out of the dark and come laughing into the light. I thank Christine Maynard, Michael Stephen, Nicholas Mandrell, Lema Lynch, Alexandra Tallent, Soleil Laboy, and Jimbo Smith and his wife, Lyndzy Goss Smith (and their daughter, Kindred). Whenever this book speaks of Jared's sensory experiences, the information most likely came from Charity Ann Williams, the inimitable Aggro, a troubadour of the rails, who all but put me in her backpack and carried me onto roaring freight trains and into stinking ravines. And, always, there was Maggie. Loving, beautiful Maggie. Maggie Fulmer and her mother, Kayla, were heroic—absolutely heroic—in giving Jared every chance to be the man we all wanted him to be.

Aggro was not alone in carrying me. Friends picked me up. In my little sportswriter world, I am a famously stubborn writer. I resist editing. I say this with no pride. It is a failing. Every writer needs a wiser person whispering into an ear, "You can do better than that." I wanted this book to be the best I could make it. I asked exceptional writers to read the work in progress and tell me how to make it sing. Thanks to the long-suffering, invaluable Gary Pomerantz. Thanks to Verenda Smith, there for me decades before Jared was born and every day since. Thanks to Jane Leavy, Tom Callahan, Billy Reed, Joan Ryan, Juliet Macur, Jeff Schultz, and John Feinstein. I bow, too, to Patti Parker. She read the manuscript in all its forms and she heard my darkest doubts as to when, if ever, I would let go of it. She finally delivered to my ass a swift, sweet kick. And here we are. Forever grateful, Ms. Parker.

The experts: First, I read David Sheff's book, every sentence and every page of *Clean: Overcoming Addiction and Ending America's Greatest Tragedy*. My understanding of the addiction tragedy profited from conversations with Jay Davidson, the administrator of an alcohol abuse facility, The Healing Place, in Louisville, Kentucky. I spoke with Sheila Levine, a mental health counselor in Nashville, Tennessee. A doctor in Michigan, Yossi Holoshitz, and a Philadelphia social worker, Deborah Lamb, cared enough about Jared to explain the desperation of his circumstances.

Hometown friends: Dave Byrne told me God stories when I needed to hear God stories. Lisa Crocker kept me smiling when there was small reason to smile. My sister, Sandra Litwiller, loved me even, or especially, when I was unlovable. The administrators, nurses, and staff at Apostolic Christian Restmor cared for my mother and then for Cheryl with 24/7/365 kindness. Early in the return to our Illinois roots, I began writing about the hometown Lady Potters. Why? Well, why not? As a big-time sports columnist I had written about every major sports event in the world. Then Cheryl and I found ourselves sitting two rows behind the players' bench at a girls' high school basketball game. Writers write, and in ten years I wrote five hundred thousand words on the Morton High School Lady Potters. Every game day, the team delivered to me a box of Milk Duds.

David Black did extraordinary work for this book as literary agent and first reader. In my early drafts, Black the first reader immediately saw a book I had not written, a better book, a grandfather's story about a grandson's story. Black the agent knew where to take the new grandfather/grandson manuscript. And here we are at PublicAffairs, embraced by publisher Clive Priddle and executive editor Benjamin Adams. Production editor Kaitlin Carruthers-Busser moved the project from manuscript to hard covers. Cindy Buck was the best of copyeditors, doing her work with a surgical precision that left the writer's fragile ego intact while improving every sentence. Julie Ford, a lawyer, protected me from legal mistakes. I thank them all.

Cheryl's heart is in every word here. This book is what she wanted it to be. A love story.

Dave Kindred has been a columnist for the *Louisville Courier-Journal*, the *Washington Post*, the *Atlanta Journal-Constitution*, the *National Sports Daily*, the *Sporting News*, and *Golf Digest*. Kindred is the author of several books, including *Heroes, Fools, and Other Dreamers: A Sportswriter's Gallery of Extraordinary People*, *Around the World in 18 Holes* (with Tom Callahan), *Morning Miracle: Inside the* Washington Post: *A Great Newspaper Fights for Its Life*, and *Sound and Fury: Two Powerful Lives, One Fateful Friendship*.

Kindred is one of only two writers who have earned sportswriting's three highest honors: the Red Smith Award, the PEN America ESPN Lifetime Achievement Award for Literary Sports Writing, and the Dan Jenkins Medal for Excellence in Sportswriting. He also has won the Naismith Memorial Basketball Hall of Fame's Curt Gowdy Award (for outstanding media contributions) as well as a National Headliner Award for general-interest columns. He is a member of the National Sports Media Hall of Fame. He lives in Illinois.

PublicAffairs is a publishing house founded in 1997. It is a tribute to the standards, values, and flair of three persons who have served as mentors to countless reporters, writers, editors, and book people of all kinds, including me.

I. F. STONE, proprietor of *I. F. Stone's Weekly*, combined a commitment to the First Amendment with entrepreneurial zeal and reporting skill and became one of the great independent journalists in American history. At the age of eighty, Izzy published *The Trial of Socrates*, which was a national bestseller. He wrote the book after he taught himself ancient Greek.

BENJAMIN C. BRADLEE was for nearly thirty years the charismatic editorial leader of *The Washington Post*. It was Ben who gave the *Post* the range and courage to pursue such historic issues as Watergate. He supported his reporters with a tenacity that made them fearless and it is no accident that so many became authors of influential, best-selling books.

ROBERT L. BERNSTEIN, the chief executive of Random House for more than a quarter century, guided one of the nation's premier publishing houses. Bob was personally responsible for many books of political dissent and argument that challenged tyranny around the globe. He is also the founder and longtime chair of Human Rights Watch, one of the most respected human rights organizations in the world.

·   ·   ·

For fifty years, the banner of Public Affairs Press was carried by its owner Morris B. Schnapper, who published Gandhi, Nasser, Toynbee, Truman, and about 1,500 other authors. In 1983, Schnapper was described by *The Washington Post* as "a redoubtable gadfly." His legacy will endure in the books to come.

Peter Osnos, Founder